The Women of Nar

The Women of Nar

JOYCE ROPER

FABER AND FABER
3 Queen Square
London

First published in 1974
by Faber and Faber Limited
3 Queen Square London WC1
Printed in Great Britain by
Latimer Trend & Company Ltd Plymouth
All rights reserved

ISBN 0 571 10445 2

© Joyce Roper, 1974

To
Katy and Sibel
with love

CONTENTS

Introduction   13

Note on Pronunciation   15

PART ONE: THE PLACE

1. I Come to Nar   19
2. The Town   31
3. Bread   38
4. Women at Work   49
5. Ceremonies   59
6. Ramazan   71
7. Festivals   80

PART TWO: THE PEOPLE

8. Pembe   87
9. Three Clans (with their family trees)   95
10. A Death   102
11. Winter Evenings   108
12. Spring; the Letter   116
13. Neziha and Nesrin   124
14. Ekrem's Wedding   132
15. The Year 1971   143
16. Pembe and İsmail   156

Conclusion   173

Note on Local Government in Rural Turkey   175

Note on Musical Instruments in the Village of Nar   176

Glossary   177

ILLUSTRATIONS

PLATES

1. Haci Baba, my landlord — *facing page* 32
2. Kazim and Gülazar. 'They were such strong, good people, always doing what they judged right in the sight of God' — 33
3. Gülten at the door to the roof — 48
4. The Meydan in winter — 49
5. 'The Primary School children . . . read their poems' (Mustafa Dede's little daughter) — 112
6. Haci Baba's granddaughter, Zelha, with a pet lamb — 113
7. 'The woman who had brought me the soup was called Ayşe' — 113
8. Pembe. 'She appeared thoughtful and sensible, a real person' — 128
9. 'Granny . . . said her rheumatism was very bad' — 128
10. The Bride. '. . . under the arches of my kitchen' — 129

MAPS

1. Turkey, showing the road to Nar village — *page* 12
2. Nar village, the lower quarter — 21

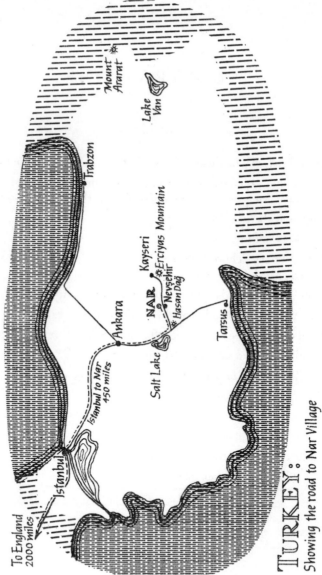

To England
2000 miles

Istanbul

Istanbul to Nar
450 miles

Salt Lake

Ankara

Trabzon

NAR
Kayseri
Nevşehir
Hasan Dağ
Erciyas Mountain

Tarsus

Mount
Ararat

Lake
Van

TURKEY:
Showing the road to Nar Village

INTRODUCTION

I have been asked why I went to live in Turkey.

At that time I had no family ties, my work as an art teacher had come to seem superficial and unsatisfactory to me and I received a legacy. I loved travel. I loved people. A chance holiday led me to Turkey where I became passionately interested in the rich and deep village culture. Because I am a woman it was possible for me to get to know the village women who cannot usually read or write; I found the language difficult to learn but not impossible. The women accepted me into their sisterhood.

The hope of promoting understanding, in however tiny a way, between nations and religions made my occasional loneliness a pleasure to endure.

My deepest thanks are due to Professor Paul Stirling of Kent University for his constructive criticism, to the Director of Tarsus Amerikan Koleji and Ruth Robeson, to Zikriye Bayrakdar of Mersin, to Harun Erdoğan of Nevşehir and above all to the women of Nar for their help and moral support in my research.

Andrew Payne prepared the prints for the plates.

J.R.

NOTE ON PRONUNCIATION

All Turkish words are pronounced as written and there are no variations to be learnt.

There are different letters: C has the sound of English J, Ç the sound of English Ch, and Ş the sound of English Sh. The undotted I is as in English 'shirt'. Ay has the sound of English long I as in 'bite', and the syllable Mey- in 'Meydan'—rhymes with English 'May'. The letter ğ is not sounded but lengthens the preceding syllable.

The most difficult word I have used is the name of the district of Nar lands called Ayağzı. This may be pronounced something like 'I-ah-ze'.

Part One

THE PLACE

I

I COME TO NAR

Damp grey April morning in Wiltshire. I move about my business in the outer everyday world, buy typing paper, go to the supermarket for necessities. Always in my mind, more real than my surroundings, is Nar, the village on the Anatolian plateau where I have spent three years.

Summer there: burning heat, bright air, cool tree shade and the pale copper-pink hillsides with their rows of green vines.

Winter: outdoors too cold for human life, red-hot stoves, sealed warm rooms and caves, people hurrying to the jolly songs and dances of wedding celebrations.

I had toured Turkey with some friends a year before I went to live there; we had met Harun, a young Town Governor. I had told him of my admiration for the villagers and my desire to study their customs. He had assured me that I could take a house in a Turkish village.

Back in England during the winter I sold my house and arranged for money to spend three years in Turkey. I studied the Turkish tapes at the Oriental Institute in Oxford, and in late spring set off with a few books and some bedding and cooking utensils in my green mini-van. I was not, am not, a sociologist, I knew nothing of the work that has been done on different cultures. Turkey has an old civilization, but a different culture and a different religion from the one I had been brought up in. It would, I thought, be like looking at an experiment of God's: give human beings two different environments in which to evolve their civilizations and see what remains constant after a couple of thousand years.

Nar.

Where is Nar?

Imagine yourself in the air looking down at Asia Minor, Anatolia

19

as it is called today. A plateau with a jumble of high peaks to the east and pine-clad ranges to the south and north. Most of the plateau is wheat-growing land, cropped one year and left fallow the next. Now, in April, as I am writing this in England, the young wheat is clothing the plateau in a green as pale and alive as light. In the middle is the great Salt Lake, the Tüz Gölü, shining silver in the sun, blackish green in shadow when clouds move over the wide sky. The lake is edged with a frill, like breakers, white, its own crystallized salt. Fifty miles to the east of it, beyond a pocking of extinct volcanic craters, the Nar valley runs north and south, and the stream fed by its many springs flows into the Kızıl Irmak, the Red River, which the ancients called the Halys. The valley is deep and emerald green, its plots of cucumbers and beans and onions and apples watered by irrigation channels.

All the surface geology in the Nar area is volcanic. The Pliocene period, perhaps three million years ago, was when most of the craters were active, spewing out ash and pumice and lava to form the pinkish hills, the basalt crags which project on the skyline and the secret valleys walled with black broken rock columns. Erciyas Dağ, fifty miles to the east, is much the highest of the extinct volcanoes; it is nearly fourteen thousand feet high and the snow on it never melts. It is always exciting to look at; from Nar a pure cone, shining white above the cloud in winter, a luminous lemon-yellow before a summer sunrise.

The village of Nar is built on a bluff of soft volcanic rock near the head of the valley, half a mile from where the stream flings itself over a basalt sill. Built into the rock, for the houses all have rooms, made ages ago perhaps, cut into the rock; now the people live most of the time in rooms built of blocks of the rock, eighteen inches long, just the right weight for a man to handle. Some rooms are arched, some roofed with poplar trunks from the tall trees which are grown all along the stream more plentifully even than the willows.

The population of Nar is about three thousand and it has a Mayor, or *Reis*, whose offices are on the Meydan. On the opposite side are the schools, fine solid buildings put up in 1960. Above the Meydan the gold-coloured minaret of the Big Mosque towers into the blue sky,

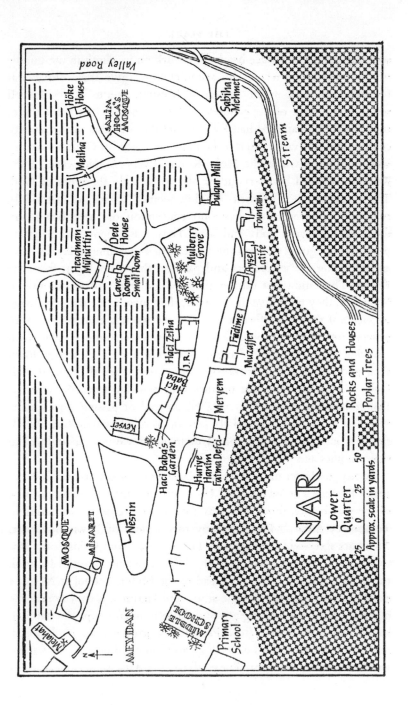

NAR
Lower Quarter
0   25   50
25
Approx. scale in yards

Rocks and Houses
Poplar Trees

scorning the green bronze head of Atatürk on its plinth in the middle of the open space where the schoolchildren give their displays at festivals. Everyone in the village is Muslim, Sunnis of the Hanefi sect. I knew little of the practice of Islam when I first went there; merely that Mohammed had lived in Southern Arabia in the seventh century and believed himself to be the mouthpiece of God; his sayings were written down as the Holy Koran. Every Arabic word of the Koran is believed by everyone in Nar to be truly the word of God. The actual practice of their religion seemed to me at first oddly materialistic, indeed they have no conception of there being any dichotomy between body and soul. They wash themselves to attain purity before going through the *namaz* ritual five times a day, bowing and repeating the set prayers and passages they have learnt from the Koran. They must fast during the daylight hours of the month of Ramazan, they must give to the poor, they must make the pilgrimage to Mecca if they can afford it . . . and the women especially have to observe lots of little prohibitions and commands, mostly to do with covering themselves before men. The recording angel writes down their good deeds and their transgressions, and, when they die, if their faults are too heavy in the balance they will fall from the Narrow Bridge into the eternal fires of Hell, instead of passing through the Narrows to Paradise. Their daily conduct is ruled by their fear of hell-fire, but in spite of that I found them good women, thoughtful to their families and their neighbours.

To my joy I met my old friend Harun as soon as I arrived in Nev-şehir. 'Find me a house quickly,' I said, and he remembered his promise of the year before, though he was now in a more important position, Temporary Assistant Province Governor instead of Town Governor. There are sixty-odd Provinces in Turkey, each comprising some five towns. All Governors belong to the Ministry of the Interior. He took me to see his friend who was Head of the Middle School at Nar; we drank glasses of tea in the little study and Harun was enormously the bigwig, graciously looking at some little Roman lamps the children had found in the vineyards. Presently a grey-haired, hook-nosed, short-bearded man in a knitted cap and loose trousers joined us and was brought a glass of tea. They talked; my Turkish was weak and I couldn't follow it all, but a bargain was concluded with the bearded man, who had a house to let which would suit me. That was how I met Haci Baba, my much respected landlord (Plate 1), who was a farmer with many scattered vineyards and gardens and orchards and wheatfields. The house was near the Meydan, on the street leading down the valley; it shared a strip of roof with Haci Baba's own.

Mine was a simple little house with no open courtyard such as most of the village houses have, but instead a crypt-like, arched-over space on the ground floor with a sink, a water-tap and a lavatory, containing a concrete hole with a foot-rest on each side. A stable and a cool storeroom were cut into the rock. Stone steps in the corner by the storeroom door led up to a little landing with doors opening on to two narrow living-rooms, facing south, whitewashed and with poplar ceilings. In winter the low sunshine streamed across the floor and warmed the rooms, but in summer, when I first arrived, the sun's rays were almost vertical and didn't reach beyond the outer window-sills. Lying on my shelf-bed by the window I could hear the cry from the mosque ringing out into the pre-dawn dark: *Allahu Ekber* . . . *Allahu Ekber* . . . *Allahu Ekber*—and the nightingales and warblers in the poplar trees would rouse themselves and start their dawn chorus, then carts would rattle along the rocky street taking whole families to field work. At five o'clock I'd lift aside the curtain to see the first sunshine of the day blazing on the rocky rim of the valley.

One day I was hanging out my washing on the roof. Gülten, Haci Baba's eldest grand-daughter, sat sewing at a cushion for her bottom drawer. Aged perhaps fourteen, mature, withdrawn, dreaming, she had remained alone in the rambling dwelling in order to prepare a meal for the rest when they came back hungry. That lovely withdrawn stillness was the poise of Turkish feminine good manners, for she asked me to join the family for their evening meal.

Ayşe, the second girl, came to fetch me. She was a year or so younger than Gülten, but rosy and glowing and forthcoming. The name Gülten means rose-flesh, it would have suited her sister better; the very popular name Ayşe is after a member of the Prophet's family. I was led through a big hall and took my shoes off outside a door which already had several pairs side by side on its threshold. The family had started eating and I was shown to a cushion on the floor by the tablecloth. On the six-inch-high table were two dishes, one of mint, lettuce and onion salad, the other of rice. I copied what they were doing, wrapping thin soft bread round pink rice and conveying it to my mouth. Haci Baba, next to me, didn't seem to be staring rudely but he must have noticed the embarrassing rice-grains I was dropping on the cloth, for he ordered a little girl to fetch me a spoon. There were two smaller girls who were going to Primary School, called Zelha and Fatik. Gülten and Ayşe had finished the five grades of Primary School; Middle School is not compulsory.

Kazim, Haci Baba's son and the children's father, finished first, got up from the floor and sat on the window-seat. Then I sat back and looked around me. The floor was covered with *kilims* and pile rugs and the walls were whitewashed. There were cupboards in the wall. There was no furniture to break up the calm space in the room, unless you count a high shelf which held a radio with a lace cover and a Holy Koran in a green one. I think it was then they told me that a Koran must never be put on a table or shelf below the level of one's navel, it would show irreverence.

Soon Kazim got up and went out to the coffee house on the Meydan, he wanted a cigarette and it is not possible for a man to smoke in front of his father, though Kazim was then in his middle forties. Right at the top of the wall I saw a photo of Haci Baba in Arab dress; he said he had had it taken at Mecca when he had made the pilgrimage, he was very proud of having been to Mecca and glad to talk about it. We went on making formal conversation for a few minutes and then Haci Baba gathered himself up and went off to a coffee house too; there were two big ones up on the Meydan, the Belediye Gazinosu and the Meydan Kiraathanesi. Both were exclusively patronized by men and I have never taken a glass of tea in either.

When Haci Baba had gone the women gathered round me, eager to try to talk. The oldest was about sixty-five, Haci Nazmiye, dark, positive in her statements, a little bossy in her manner to the other two grown women. Yet she had only been married to Haci Baba for a year or two. When his first wife, the mother of Kazim and a handsome middle-aged woman called Taybe, had died, inquiries had been made for a replacement and they had heard of Nazmiye, a widow, the mother of a greengrocer in Nevşehir, who had been trying to live with her daughter-in-law there. She was authoritative, especially with Gülazar Hanım, the elder of Kazim's two wives. I didn't think it always went down too well, and Gülazar didn't speak freely in front of Haci Nazmiye, who was theoretically in the position of mother-in-law to her. But usually Gülazar would go straight up to women visitors who didn't know her, and make her position clear. She had married Kazim, Haci Baba's son and heir, when she was a beautiful and strong girl with a good endowment of desirable gardens. But after ten years they had had no children. According to ancient custom another, junior, bride must be sought. Gülazar agreed to young Nazmiye coming into the household as a second wife, with no dowry; she was proud to be the second wife in such a respected household. It is very confusing to write about, for there were two Nazmiyes in the family, the elder, sixty-five, always being called Haci Nazmiye. The younger, thirty-five, was always called Little Mother by the children, while Gülazar Hanım was called Big Mother. When I got to know them all I felt that the children were extremely lucky to have two such mothers.

But Gülazar was sad that God had not given her any children; you could see it in her burning black eyes. I respected her and her husband Kazim deeply, they were such strong, good people, always doing what they judged right in the sight of God (Plate 2).

When Haci Baba had gone off to the coffee house, Gülazar and Nazmiye and the girls took me into a room with a big brass bedstead in it on the other side of the hall. The electric light was dim, a fifteen-watt bulb perhaps, and they pulled out boxes of clothes and gave me some green *dimi* to put on, full trousers. I peered at myself in a tilted horizontal mirror hung up at ceiling level, and it didn't seem like me at all, I haven't a slim girl's waist and my legs are long, too long for the *dimi*. My dreams of romantic Arabian Nights pantaloons faded. Actually the *dimi*, the working and street dress of all Nar women, are different from the *şalvar* worn by both sexes in the south. *Dimi* are made of four metres of thick cotton stuff, sewn into a wide sack, with holes at the two bottom corners bound with a good piece of material from an old pair. The waist is bound with a strip wide enough to hold a heavy cord, and that's it. They are worn over a dress, the skirt of which is folded up neatly to go into them. A knitted waistcoat is worn over the dress, a butter muslin square, folded into a triangle, is placed over the hair and, with a corner held in each hand, is folded over the face and tucked in to cover the nose and mouth. For going about the village or for riding a donkey to field work a big white cotton sheet, spotlessly laundered, is put over the head, falling to calf length behind. In a field it will be put, carefully folded, on a tree branch; in a neighbour's house it will be taken off and folded up or hung up somewhere. But for visiting town or for grand occasions, it is replaced by a big brown shawl of fine wool. It isn't as lovely as the white sheet, and I asked a woman going to a wedding why she wore it, in the heat of summer too, and she replied that it was '*Moda*', in fashion. I think she was disappointed that I didn't admire it.

I hated myself in the *dimi*, and I couldn't walk with all the fullness between the legs. I felt like a prolapsed cow and never wore them again. But they are decent for work, the women and girls climb trees to gather cherries and apples in them, and of course you can sit cross-legged comfortably.

After we had looked at the clothes, they lit a little lamp, saying '*Bismillah Irrahman Irrahim*', 'In the Name of God the Compassionate, the Merciful', as they touched the match to the wick, and took me into the hill to see their cave storerooms.

Beside half-a-dozen piled sacks of flour at the end of the hall was the entrance to the caves. On one side I saw piles of folded carpets reaching to the roof, with next to them stacks of rolled mattresses stuffed with warm wool. On the other side rank upon rank of yard-high Ali Baba jars leaned against each other, with wooden covers, full of ground wheat, home-made noodles, dried apricots, pickled peppers, pickled gherkins, grape syrup, cakes of grape syrup and wheat called *tarhan*, sweets made of grape syrup thickened with home-made wheat starch and then dried in the sun, called *koftır*. Walnuts from the groves down the valley, apples, pears, and quinces were piled around, sunflower seeds, maize for popping at winter parties . . . food, enough and to spare, to stand a winter's siege. Sometimes it would be a bad year for apricots and plums, a late frost would spoil the blossom, or, worst of all, drought would reduce the wheat crop to famine level. Then those tons of raisins in the corner would sustain life in Nar and the other vine-growing villages. Perhaps not tons of raisins, tons of grapes, rather for they are reduced at least a third in weight by drying. A ton in Turkey, spelt the same, weighs nearly the same as a ton in England. In Turkish it is pronounced to rhyme with the English word 'don'.

I can't remember half the things in jars in the cave; hemp seeds to roast with wheat in the winter, pumpkin and melon seeds to salt and roast, and most important to Haci Baba, seeds for all the next year's crops.

The little lamp flickered as we passed the stacks of bedding; its light caught a rosy gleam from stacked cauldrons and huge baths and trays of copper, lined with tin. Equipment for more than one household was there in the shadows; copper utensils are bought by weight and taken to the tinner for the inside to be plated with tin. Each bride must have a set of such equipment. Then there were sieves made of cow gut, tall baskets for grapes, and in the shadowy corners, all the sickles and shovels and ploughs for the farm.

As we came back through the hallway I looked into the room we had had our meal in and saw the three smallest children, Mehmet and Zelha and Fatik, lying asleep on the floor with their heads on their mother's lap, radiating out from her, an enchanted star.

At the door to the roof (Plate 3), I peered for the steps, for darkness had long fallen, and Gülten handed me a posy of geranium, sweet william, and scented leaves. 'İyi geceler, Allah rahatlık versin,' 'Goodnight, may God give you rest,' and I went in to bed and lay down thoughtfully, watching the moonlight streaming through the curtains.

Everything was so strange, how was I to get to know these people? It was to take me a long time to fit the jangling elements of village life together and see how they made a harmonious whole.

The very word 'village' is misleading to English ears, suggesting a scattered group of dwellings for retired townspeople and a few agricultural workers, where everyone's life is what he himself chooses to make it. In English villages the bond of church life has loosened and the pubs are taken over by motorists. Much more than that, the

English village is not of great importance in the structure of national and political life.

On the other hand, seventy per cent of Turks live in villages and most of the rest visit their native village for holidays. A village is a close-knit and self-supporting community, one which is able to shake off empires like water off a duck's back. It is usually well governed. Political theorists say a town or country or the world cannot in the nature of things be as well governed as a village, a 'cannot' ruling which if I were young I should consider a barrier worth breaking, a more exciting and worth-while objective than visiting the moon.

Of course there is always the possibility of war, or at least a state of unarmed hostility, with the next village. One day I was sitting reading in the shade by a lovely stream where it forms the village boundary. The Nar men working in their gardens nearby kept coming out into the trackway to see that I was all right and not being spoken to or molested by those strangers from the neighbouring village.

And I must explain something about this book now; simply that nothing of what I say about Nar must be taken as necessarily applying to another village. As a small example, the Avanos women twenty kilometres away wear beautiful purple and red shawls to weddings, whereas ours wear dull brown wool—and as for men, well, those of Çat, the village immediately west of Nar, are fantastically quick with gun or knife, as well as loving horses.

The most difficult thing to understand is the conflict between civil and religious law. Even Nar people don't find this easy; they love to do what is right but to know it often needs thought and discussion. According to the civil law a man may have only one wife: a good and respected village woman gave me her opinion of a man who was thinking of taking a second wife, unrecognized in law.

'It is an unmannerly thing to do; she could not have any legal position or rights, therefore he is not thinking of her real interests in proposing such a thing. If he were a good man (i.e. a good Muslim) he would put the matter out of his mind.'

The Muslim religious law was the law of the Ottoman Empire, except for the minority communities, Jews, Christians, French, and so on. The civil law for everyone, based on Italian and Swiss models, was introduced by Kemal Atatürk, who pulled a territorially diminished Turkey out of the wreck of the Empire after the First World War. He introduced many reforms to enable Turkey to deal on equal terms with western countries. The Latin alphabet and the western solar calendar were brought in suddenly, men and women were to be legally equal, there was to be compulsory primary education for all boys and girls, everyone had to take a surname, men must not wear the fez, women should not wear veils.

Unfortunately Atatürk died before women were really free or a true democracy had been established, and the pace of reform is very slow. Men and women aren't exactly equal in Nar. Women and girls are loved and protected and it is the pride of the men to love and protect them. Boys, on the other hand, are given everything they want from birth, and their opinions deferred to even by their mothers because of their superior sex. Suddenly, at the age of fifteen, they are not allowed to speak to girls any more, hardly to see them, certainly not to look at them; to ogle them we should call it. Such is the force of an established custom that they don't become psychotic. In a year or two, before they become liable for military service at twenty, the father will look round for money for a bride-price and the mother will make inquiries about any suitable girls, looking for one who is a virgin, one who will be a devoted servant and companion for herself, and able to bear children. The inquiries are conducted delicately, but since the choice of a first cousin cuts out the necessity for asking around, this practice is much favoured.

There are no social occasions where boys and girls may get to know each other, but little groups of boys, and even of girls, dress very smartly to walk into town to school or to work in a bank or office. Though they don't apparently stare across at them they are presumably aware of each other in the distance. When a girl has had an engagement arranged for her by the two families, she may shake the groom's hand at a party, then she is veiled for ever from the world and is heavily covered when she must go into the street. But an open court is hers to work in, and possibly a breezy flat roof with geraniums or roses in pots on it. In summer, the Nar women work in the fields, with the mid-day meal often a family picnic.

They had had a very good reason for the second wife in Haci Baba's family. There were other two-wife families in Nar, some dating from before Atatürk's reforms. Our good headman, Mühüttin Bey, had two who looked after him devotedly when he was ill; he died of hardening of the arteries in the winter of 1971–2. Our Health Officer had two wives dating from before the reform, but they both looked sad.

In other places a second wife was taken more lightly. I heard of a family with eight children who had moved from a village to a town and had more money. The wife was lonely and overworked and begged her man to take another wife. He asked the children if they would mind and they said not, if it was what their mother wanted, so an extremely nice woman was found. They were all happy. The husband spent two nights with one and two nights with the other with unbroken regularity. Number one said that the arrangement didn't hurt her heart at all, indeed she felt very sorry for number two when she had to sleep alone for she had no children to keep her company. That seems to me to be an odd but genuine example of Christian thoughtfulness for one's neighbour. Another house was unfortunate. There the man's mother ruled the roost; though the woman had fine sons the mother said she wanted more help with the outdoor work and a Circassian girl was bought. The man was reluctant at first, but what happened was that the two women quarrelled every night outside his door about whose turn it was to sleep with him. They lived in a flat, the neighbours were disturbed by the noise and the ménage was not held in high esteem; I saw the man one day in a shop with an unholy twinkle in his eye.

The Nar people were very good to me. I awakened to a deeper happiness every day, as the virtuous and splendid women accepted me into their sisterhood, and the lonely misery of my first weeks was forgotten. Harun, the English-speaking official who had made it possible for me to live in Nar, had gone to do his military service, eighteen months or two years in the army, which all men must do before they are forty. I was left to paddle my own canoe, and did it with delight.

2

THE TOWN

Scent of the oleaster flowers, warm, sweet, musky, clean . . . like a child's sunwarmed flesh. In June the scent of the greenish-yellow flowers blows over the Nevşehir road, where in winter the stinking Bacchic wine-lees run puce-pink down the rock from the wine-factory. Children's footprints in the sand by the roadside, each toe-print a crisp intaglio.

I am walking up to the town market this summer day and groups of women are going up the hill too; the two kilometres to town only takes half an hour. Soft-footed they pad along, wide bottoms swaying in enormously full trousers, white veils fluttering to knee level, faces tight-wrapped in muslin. Curiosity, a friendly look, but I can't recognize them.

'What are you doing? Where are you going?'

'I am going to Nevşehir. What are you doing?'

'We too are going to Nevşehir.'

Sting of stones thrown by a scutter of small boys, one or two hitting my legs. I am interested to discover in myself the slight sadness, the out-of-touchness, of any alien minority; to them I was an infidel, a woman alone, outcast.

A turn in the road and there in front is the battlemented castle on its hill, all dimmed with the morning haze; in front of it the minarets to the north of the town with their lacy balconies stand out, sharply black.

The market crowd thickens. Peasant women crowned with coins, dressed in crimson and scarlet printed cotton, slide like well-trained dogs after their menfolk; the women carry heavy donkey bags stuffed with all the goods they are to sell or have bought. One over there sits on the kerb nursing her swaddled babe, the end of her firmly-tied

face veil floating loose over her bare breast. Neat teenagers go down to
the Lycée, boys and girls in separate groups, crisp and collected, their
books under their arms.

I want to buy fruit, meat and bread, perhaps to see my friend
Harun's mother. Or to sit with my friend Zikriye Hanım in the
pharmacist's shop where she helps her husband on market day, and
watch the patient villagers come in. Perhaps a Kurdish bride, slender
and fiery in scarlet and purple, hung with gold, with face unveiled and
with a high headdress. Or the stout middle-aged man in western
clothes who is buying a pair of rubber baby pants.

'Why doesn't his wife come in and buy such things?'

'My wife has no time, she has the horse out in the fields ploughing
the fallow and she must get it done.'

I go to look for yoğurt in the Butter Market, where buckets and
tins and piles of dairy stuff of all kinds are laid out on long communal
concrete counters.

'I want some full-fat yoğurt. Where is it?'

'Here, here, how good it is.' He made the gesture indicating superla-
tive deliciousness, finger-tips together, palm up.

'Taste it', holding out a hunk on a huge knife.

I tasted and it was good.

'Very good, I want one kilo.'

'Where is that lazy plastic bag seller? Boy, boy, come here!'

For a penny or two I bought a bag, and my kilo of delicious creamy
sweet yoğurt was put in it and weighed and delivered into my basket
with a polite salutation.

Up to the fruit market, past the fur-sellers, who sometimes have the
skins of animals of zoological interest, an otter or a red deer, often
grey wolves and fawn-brown foxes. At a shop selling carpets I may
ask the price of one to take home to England. I shall not go for years
but the price will not fall. The trouble is to find one I like, all the dyed
wool ones are too bright, I must buy one of natural wool in brown
and cream and white.

In the fruit market I go first to Haci Nazmiye's son for some peaches;
his stall has lettuce, parsley, tomatoes, cucumber, peppers—there are
some peaches but they are the white ones, the flesh doesn't come off

1. Haci Baba, my landlord

2. Kazim and Gülazar. 'They were such strong, good people, always doing what they judged right in the sight of God'

the stones easily. Oh, there they are, the golden furry ones, up from the coast that morning on a lorry, the box hardly started.

'Two kilos of those, please, Mustafa.'

'Very good. How is my mother?'

'She is well, working hard.'

'What a woman for work, never happy unless she is hard at it.'

The butchers' shops are near the fruit market, all close together round the central court with a water tap, where the beasts are killed. I hate the meat market, but a cat has come to live with me and I have to buy a set of liver and lights and heart and kidneys which the cat and I share; she has the lights and heart. The sets, as they are called, are hung in disgusting bunches at the door of a booth.

'How much is the set?'

'Twelve and a half.' (Turkish lira are thirty-six to the pound sterling.)

'Goodness, it's gone up since last week.'

'It's the tourist season starting, there is more demand from the hotels.'

'This is a good one, the liver a good colour, but it has only one kidney, in England the sheep have two kidneys.'

'The killer always takes one kidney.'

'I'll give ten.'

'It cannot be.'

'Ten,' firmly.

'Eleven,' sadly.

'Very good, I'll take it.'

'Why don't you become a Muslim?'

'Why don't you become a Christian?'

Now really shocked, looking up pop-eyed:

'It CANNOT be.'

One day I needed plates. Turkish guests were coming and it was all right for us to sit on the floor, but I hadn't enough plates, or the shallow bowls they serve the food in if they do present individually and not in a communal dish. A Nar girl was married to a Nevşehir man and I went to see her to ask which was the best shop to buy plates.

She fixed her veil and her big brown shawl and led me out into a

C   33

quiet back street and down some steps to a door which a woman opened in answer to our knocking. We were led into a cellar store-room where there were stacks of enamel pots and plastic plates and bowls. I hastily chose three plain plates which would do. I wanted to live as simply as possible and not buy anything that was not an absolute necessity. But that furtive way of shopping is forced by custom on the Nevşehir women; I would have been happier inspecting the display in a showroom, where they, on the other hand, would feel un-comfortable.

I went to the shop which sold typing paper, but alterations were in progress and I was led to a side-street shop where the stock had been piled on the floor. I sat waiting; sitting waiting is a favourite Turkish occupation and it's a thing you have to like. Presumably the paper was on its way, and the man who had led me there asked me if he could bring a friend to talk to me.

'Of course.'

A dignified well-fed man with beard and skull-cap appeared, with a certain unworldly careless disorder in his dress. He seated himself opposite me, where the light from the shop-door fell on his serious face.

'Why don't you become a Muslim and go to Paradise?'

He was intelligent and probably well read. I told him the gist of E. M. Forster's short story about the Christian and the Muslim who die and wait outside the Gate of Paradise together, each sincerely hoping the other may get in and not thinking about himself at all. Both are let in, the Muslim finding himself in a garden full of identical and nubile houris, the Christian finding himself issued with a white robe and a harp which he must learn to play. Both become very bored, both are let out again straight into the eternal radiance of God. In the story they both become part of the great world soul, but I thought that a difficult idea and anyhow I don't know the Turkish for it. I don't know whether he understood the story or not, he didn't admit incomprehension, but rose and retired with proper salutations.

The main road from the west to the tourist centre at Göreme and Ürgüp runs through Nevşehir; on the south side are shops, and on the north the large and slightly bleak and official Government Buildings, including the police headquarters and the land office. Beside them is what is known as the Park, a garden-like space where women may be served with tea or cold drinks in summer.

I sit with my grape juice and look at the equestrian statue of Kemal Atatürk in front of the Government building. It is very pleasing to me, and is a massive enough shape to hold its own in the centre of the volcanic hills ringing the town. It is carved of golden-brown stone and in order to make it strong and able to stand, the sculptor has made the legs very thick indeed, so that it is a truly great horse, ready for a tourney. To Muslims, representational sculpture is even worse than paintings of people—the legend of course is that God will require the artist to give his representations breath or he will be thrown into hell. I drew the women when I first went to Nar, but they liked this practice less and less and I had to take to photography which they knew simply recorded light.

Atatürk set his face against this superstition and the equestrian statue is one of the fruits of his reforms. In my eyes, it comes off. But the other big statue nearby is unfortunate, a slightly larger-than-life bronze of İbrahim Paşa the Bridegroom, a local boy who made good by becoming minister to a Sultan and marrying his daughter. His statue would be lovely were it small, a foot high, when its naturalism would be charming and agreeable, but there he is like a dark-brown Father Christmas in his long robes and high hat; the only thing to do with him would be to paint him red and his beard white like his fellow Anatolian, St. Nicholas. He doesn't require a statue for a memorial in Nevşehir, for the library and the baths he built there in the eighteenth century are still in use, and the present museum was his theological school. And of course the great lead-roofed mosque in the same group of buildings as the library and museum was his gift too. I've never been inside the mosque but the tight mass of domes and minaret is very fine. The lavatories in the mosque court I have been to, they also are eighteenth century and spotlessly clean.

Everything any villager could want is displayed for sale in the Nevşehir Monday market; an open space is full of stalls and men with cloths spread on the ground, selling knives and rope and socks and hand-block printed tablecloths and carpets and *kilims* and bowls; the furnishing stuffs outdazzle even the red and blue and yellow prints for the village women's dresses.

I was bargaining for a printed tablecloth one day when Harun's aunt appeared at my elbow and brought the price down by ten lira. Once Harun's mother had wanted slippers; her bargaining was without success and she came towards me with disgust for the salesman audible in her voice:

'İnmedi.' 'He didn't come down.'

I never learnt to bargain well, it is a game, one of the few permitted to women.

Village women whose husbands are working in Germany bring their donkeys to market and take back meat in hundredweights; they fry it up in its own fat in wide copper pans and put it in earthenware jars with fat on top, just as they do with the cows killed at home. It keeps for months. The earthenware jars they use, the water-jars stacked at that street corner over there, and the tall jars, are all made at the potteries at Avanos, by the Kızıl Irmak, the Red River, twenty kilometres away. They are fired in huge kilns using chaff and sawdust; clouds of black smoke rise when a kiln is lit at dawn, and by nightfall an adequate temperature of perhaps 1,000° C. is reached. The water-jars are all the same size and are used as measures, their name, *testi*, is Latin so probably they have been made and used here since Roman times.

I buy my bread last, at the baker's on the corner. The baker gives me the kind of loaf he knows I like, with the sweetest of smiles. I had to make it a rule in Turkey not to speak to men, but sometimes down the valley road a man would hand me two of his best tomatoes or a beautiful apple as though I were a great lady.

The luckiest day for me was the day the pharmacist insisted I speak to his wife on the telephone; Zikriye Hanım's English is perfect though she has not spoken it in everyday life for thirty years; she was educated at an American Presbyterian school at Adana in South-east Turkey. She speaks Arabic and Persian even more fluently, as well as her native Turkish. She is brilliant at understanding other people's problems, and helped me all the time; her two daughters adore her, and also her two lovely little grandsons. One day she came to visit me in Nar and as she was returning on the minibus she got into conversation with a village elder who told her that I, her friend Sevinç Hanım (as they always called me, Sevinç is a usual name meaning Joy), was worth five village women. I felt ashamed when Zikriye Hanım told me that, because the village women are brave and practical and really belong, truly they are the salt of the earth, they are worth five of me.

But I am proud that the village elders like me.

3

BREAD

The piece of dry bread spun through the air into the open front of the stove. I looked up at my guests to see if they were ready to start the meal.

Two pairs of wide horrified eyes looked at me.

Zikriye said, scarcely able to be polite:

'Bread is a holy thing, you must never throw it away, you must never burn it. It is God's gift. You must kiss it and touch it to your forehead and put it somewhere where it may feed birds or animals.'

Again Zikriye had taught me a local custom. I never threw bread away again. I had thought that piece too dry to set before guests.

Bread is indeed the staff of life. Each village household grows its own wheat, and the senior man and woman in a household are always aware of the position in regard to it. Gülazar, the senior wife of Haci Baba's son Kazim, the childless one, always knew the height of the stacks of bread in the cave, always knew the state of the sacks of flour piled at the back of the hallway; knew, too, how the wheat growing through the winter was responding to the weather. It is the same in every true village family in Nar.

I went with a rather poor family to sow wheat in October—the verb for 'sow', ek, must be related to Ekim, the word for October. Two girls and I stooped to pick up the lumps of basalt scattering the surface and threw them on to the long pile, the result of centuries of cultivation, along the edge of the tilled soil. Tiring work, the weather was still hot, and the weight of the stones made our bodies swing. They were wearing full trousers and the younger, Pembe, had a kerchief tied under her chin. The other was married and had a veil over her nose. The field was on a stony hilltop on the other side of the green valley from Nar. During the fallow year the basalt fragments had come up in quantities through the pinkish pumice sand. As we worked we looked out of the corner of our eyes to where a boy was struggling to plough the stony soil with an old white horse. The ploughshare would hook under a stone and he'd have to heave the heavy thing out and over. The horse strained forward and turned and turned in a circle as it came to the middle of the patch they were doing. The boy did the two longish pieces of land in separate patches, not ploughing along but round and round. His father had a white bag at his waist with seed wheat in it and he sowed each patch after we had cleared the worst stones off and before the boy ploughed it. He hurled the seed with a twist of the wrist so that each grain penetrated the soil. When all the seed had been covered by the ploughing it would be left to the winter rains, to lie under a blanket of snow, to respond quickly to the hot spring sun, to fill its ears in the rains of May and to be harvested in June or July.

One year there had been very little snow or rain in the winter. The soil was dry and the wheat plants at the end of April were yellowing off without having produced any ears. On a Saturday evening word came round the village that we were to pray for rain at dawn next day up on the hill. They said I could go too.

At the dawn call to prayer at around four I looked out into the dark street. Two houses across the way showed warmly lit windows; I dressed quickly, went to join Fadime and Muzaffer, the housewives from over the road, and we walked up across the Meydan. By that time the eastern sky was visibly greying. Fadime said:

'Have you a prayer for rain in your Good Book? We have none.'

'Yes,' I replied.

'Go and get it quickly, we'll wait here for you.'

I ran down the hill, found my old prayer book, and puffed back to join them again. I smiled a bit because it seemed impossible that such a prayer should ever be needed in England. But there it was; perhaps the climate of England has deteriorated since the seventeenth century.

When we got to the top of the hill next to the village cemetery we joined a group of women, like pale moths in their white *çarsafs*, their sheet veils. I was told that they wanted me to read my prayer. I sat on a rock which had tumbled from the cemetery wall and opened the book on my knee; I was shaking and my hands were sweaty and I also felt embarrassed; stupidly because the lack of bread would endanger our lives and it was up to me to do what I could. But the women listened reverently. I read it three times in a low voice.

'Send us, we beseech thee, in this our necessity, such moderate rain and showers that we may receive the fruits of the earth to our comfort and to Thy honour.' I said '*Amin*' at the end with the long 'ee' in the second syllable, and they joined in. We were all thinking of the little wheat plants sticking forlornly out of the dry ground, and of times in the past when there had been no flour in the sacks and none to be bought.

Across the hill there were two or three hundred men wearing knitted caps or tweed ones put on back to front. A few teenagers were bareheaded. On our side some sheep bleated most pitifully, their shepherd had left them and gone to pray with the men. A man stood up facing the rest and began to recite the Koran, his voice thin and clear.

As the sun lifted over the eastern hills more men streamed up from the big mosque where they had been praying. The Hoca, the religious teacher, came with them in a white turban with a red top; his black overcoat was dignified and he had a fine beak of a nose, but the effect was spoilt in my eyes by the white stubble on his chin. He prayed for a while and all of us said '*Amin*' at the right places. Another man stood up with a piece of paper from which he read a special prayer for rain. Then he told us all to take off our coats and put them on again inside out. Muzaffer wriggled about under her sheet until she had got her cardigan off and on again; other women like Fadime just turned their sheets, they looked the same but God would know. Meryem without any nonsense took off her sheet, turned her woolly waistcoat and put the sheet over the top of her head again. I took off my jacket and put it on again with the shiny grey lining outwards, the tailor's label prominently displayed at the back of the neck. Most of the men's jackets were like that too.

Then the prayer leader told us to hold out our hands palm down with the fingers pointing towards the dry earth, a sign to God that we wanted rain. (Signs, by the way, are always considered more respectful than spoken words.)

Some minutes of that and it was time for the prayer ritual, the *namaz*. Men and women took off their shoes and prayed, first standing, then bending, then kneeling, putting their heads in the dust to the sound of the leader's '*Allahu Ekber*', 'God most great'. I sat beside the women, my sisters, in their bare feet or patched stockings, for shoes are removed for prayer. At the end of each *raket* or prayer sequence they swayed and turned their heads first to the right, then to the left, for the moving '*Esselamun aleikum ve rahmet ullah,*' the salute to the neighbours. The long white sheets in their fluted folds swayed too.

We knew rain would come.

The sun was already leaping up from the horizon but it brought a strong cold wind from the north-west. I was tired and felt out of my depth. I walked down very slowly with the two women, slowly because we were behind some doddering old men and it would be unseemly for women to pass a man. Time had stopped moving, I wasn't hungry though I had eaten nothing.

That afternoon the sky clouded over but very little rain came, perhaps three drops. On Monday it poured all afternoon and again on Tuesday. On Wednesday it soaked down steadily and heavily all day. Next morning I stood on the roof and listened; the valley was humming with birdsong and the dripping of leaves and the water-sound of myriads of little brooks. I could hardly distinguish the deeper note of the stream though it was in spate. The vineyards on the hillside were a damp copper colour, dotted with the emerald jewels of the vines.

That afternoon I found my friend Melek Hanım weeding her onion seedlings in her garden by the brook. I stopped to help her and she told me to leave the few cabbage seedlings but to weed out the radishes from the straight-leaved onions. I couldn't tell radish from cabbage and we laughed. Fadime came up and joined in our laughter and said:

'God accepted our prayers, didn't he?'

She picked a flower of pink salsify and touched the stalk running with milky juice, first to her own cheek, and then to mine. As it dried, the juice left dark grey-brown freckles.

'They're called Anatolian beauty spots. Come along and I'll give you some leeks.'

We walked quickly through knee-high nettles in a grove where a nightingale was singing full-throated at half-past-two in the afternoon. In the leek garden I looked up at the walnut trees overhanging rocky terraces; the tuff pinnacles like improbable illustrations to a fairy tale were decorated with yard-high spikes of pink Jerusalem sage and clumps of yellow St. John's wort. She dragged an armful of leeks from the black soil, tied them with a fibrous weed that seemed to be growing there for that purpose and presented them to me.

That year the rains were not heavy, but they were sufficient, and there was enough wheat for everyone to have plenty of bread.

At the end of June when the weather was blazingly hot, Haci Baba decided to harvest his wheat. Very early in the morning we set off in the cart, going down the valley as far as Soğukpınar, the Cold Spring, then up to the main road and along it, perhaps ten kilometres from Nar, to the area called Ayağzi, Moonmouth, where the whitish-pink dust scattered with lumps of rock looked like the surface of the moon. We turned off the road and bumped over a track to where the green vines and the golden wheat were flourishing in the volcanic soil.

At noon I rested in the shade of an apricot tree. My arms were pricked and bleeding from the armfuls of wheat I had been cutting and carrying. No wonder the women were working in two thicknesses of long-sleeved upper garments. The ordinary village woman's clothes are working clothes; God made her for work and she dresses accordingly. I looked out from the cool at them still going steadily to and fro like columns of dusty light in the hot air, their height exaggerated by the flatness of the field and the wideness of the huge plateau view beyond them. The wheat was either pulled by hand, root and all, or cut by a sickle. The women had only one little sickle between them. The wheat was laid in heaps roughly as big as one woman could carry, roots together, ears together, then it was carried over to where Haci Baba was supervising the building of a stack with the roots outside; a stack only breast-high for each bundle was packed in place by hand, we had no pitchforks or anything to lift them with. The earth was carefully shaken from the roots as they left the dry powdery soil.

We had had breakfast almost as soon as we arrived at the wheatfield. Gülazar had frizzled some pieces of fatty meat in a shallow pan and added tomato sauce and fresh tomatoes. When it was almost done she poured in water from an earthenware jar and broke six eggs into it and poached them. We ate dipping the thin bread into it and it was very good indeed.

Haci Baba had hired a day labourer from a wheat-growing village. He used a long sickle and cut all the stalks evenly. After the meal he smoked a cigarette and we looked at his set of finger guards, three of them, one each for the middle, fourth and little fingers of the left hand. These encircled the wheat to be cut by the sickle so the guards were necessary. The guards or *enik* were made of tinplate and extended two inches beyond the finger tips, ending in a broad claw.

When we'd had breakfast it was obvious that the day was going to be very hot indeed and people took off all the clothes they could spare while still conforming to their very rigorous standards of decency. Gülten, the eldest daughter, took off her everyday *dimi* and put on an old pair. Then she had a better idea and took the old ones off again to remove the long pantalettes which she had embroidered herself in red. On went the old *dimi* again over her short drawers, she tucked her dress in, did up the drawstring, put on old patched socks and cheap plastic slippers and was ready for work. Haci Baba was only wearing a loose cotton undershirt and loose long white underdrawers; with the coloured handkerchief he had wound round his head he looked like a pirate. The older women didn't think it proper to take off any clothes for work, in spite of the heat. The children weren't bothered by thoughts of propriety and ran about in cotton dresses and underdrawers of floral print.

After breakfast and the other meals Gülazar did the washing-up Arab-style, with sand and vineleaves, finishing up with a rinse from the water-jar; then off she went into the sunny field where she worked harder than anyone. I worked too, carrying bundles to the stack. One of the women got a rope from the cart and tied each end of it round a huge bundle of wheat, then we lifted each bundle on to a woman's back and they staggered over to the stack. They found that saved time and repeated it for an hour or two. I ran quickly over with my smaller armfuls, hurrying lest they spill in disorder before I placed them on the stack.

As I walked back empty-handed I saw a big coffee-coloured grass-hopper on Gülten's hair. It was a God's Camel, they all said, and mustn't be hurt or killed. Innocent-seeming columns of dust moved over the plain, but one such little whirlwind in its invisible dance snatched up half our stack into the air and scattered it. Those swirling columns of hot air are called Blind Devils, *Kör Şeytan*.

Haci Baba was old-fashioned in making exclusive use of woman-power while the horses rested in the shade. Another family I worked with loaded the wheat into a horse-drawn cart which a girl led up and down. All through the long afternoon it got hotter and hotter, more and more Blind Devils danced, and beyond them the mountain peak shimmered in the haze. At half-past five only the wheat in the last corner of the field was left standing, the sun was going behind the peak and Haci Baba said that was enough, they could do the rest when they came out with the threshing-machine in a day or two. He paid off the labourer who then strode off in the direction of his village. The women all began to pray, first performing their ritual ablutions with water from a little spouted jar. When they had done we got into the cart and went home through the twilight, Gülazar jumping off when we were going uphill to make it easier for the horse. I sat on the back, looking down at her shapely feet kicking up the donkey-dung as she strode along the road-edge. At home a girl brought me food for supper and when I had eaten it I took back the dish, to find that they had all fallen asleep where they sat. Haci Baba slowly came awake and I thanked him for my enjoyable day in the field.

'Elbostan wheat,' he said sleepily. 'Ought to yield twice as well in a good year.'

He dragged himself to his feet to do his bed-time *namaz* and I went over to my house to bed.

He was going to get the threshing-machine to do his wheat, but in that, Nar is very modern. The old way, still used in other villages, is to put the cut wheat on a stone threshing-floor, harness beasts to a board studded with flint teeth, and drive them round and round over the wheat for a day or two. A horse or a couple of donkeys or cows may provide the motive power, and anyone in the family who isn't doing anything else stands or sits on the board and steers it round and round. I boldly tried with a horse and donkey; I thought that as the beasts had already been doing it for a day they would know their way round the circle, but not at all, my fine pair wove about as though drunk, and I had to think more about keeping my balance than steering them. I was laughed off after a round or two, but little children, or granny, or anyone, can do it well. When all the straw is small and the grain freed from the ear it's ready for the winnowing, the separation of the grain from the chaff or short straw. For that the wind is used. The threshing-floor is always on the top of a hill or in the windiest spot available. The cut straw and grain mixture has to be thrown up against the wind hour after hour, until the heavy grain has fallen into a pile on the ground while the lighter straw has been blown into a much bigger contiguous pile. The implement for throwing the wheat up into the wind is beautiful, like a huge wooden hand a foot across, a concave shovel with five fingers made from one piece of tough wood, beech or hornbeam; it's called a *yaba*. Anyone strong and active, either man or woman, does the winnowing.

Today in the bigger places contractors take round threshing-machines; the women say they leave fewer stones to be picked out. In the wide wheatfields near the Salt Lake the contractors have combine harvesters which they take round; the huge unlit machines move from farm to farm along the roads at night. Money earned in German factories may be invested in such a machine.

The women and children must pick the grain free of stones immediately, before it is taken to the mill to be ground. Our family sit around a continually renewed pile of golden wheat for eight days, picking out the grey pumice fragments. They choose the end of the hallway with a view over my roof for that monotonous job. When the wheat is clean it is taken to the mill down the valley to be ground into flour. The mill itself is not old, its builder told me about its structure, but it is of a very old type indeed; there are several ancient ruined ones up the valley as well as one other in use. The water to turn it is led down a channel from the stream to an almost vertical pit four feet square at the top and sixteen metres deep. The pit is much smaller at the bottom where the water is forced under great pressure through a still smaller hole on to the vanes of a turbine which turns the vertical rod fixed to the upper, rotating millstone. The lower millstone is fixed. The grain is put into a wooden hopper which feeds it into the middle of the upper stone and it comes out at the side between the stones as warm, sweet-smelling flour. The miller shovelled some into a cloth for me to take home and make into bread; it was warm between my hands, almost as though it were alive. There were old millstones round the mill chamber with a pattern of channels on them similar to those on English millstones. The miller was a patient and saintly little man who sat still all day, with his tobacco and his water-jar on a cushion beside him, and a rope by his hand with which he could make adjustments to the flow of the wheat into the hole in the wheel. The vaulted roof was hung with flour-whitened cobwebs. The water-jet roared out at the side of the mill after it had turned the wheel. The mayor of Nar owned the mill, the miller was his employee.

As soon as the new flour comes back from the mill our family make a batch of thin *yufka* bread. No yeast is used and this is the recipe:

> Three sacks of flour
> Fourteen jars of water
> Five kilos of salt

Five households join in the making; bread is made in each of the houses in turn and each household works for the house in which the bread is being made—that is, the flour used belongs to the house the bread is made in and the woman of that house, in our case Gülazar, mixes the dough. She did this bit by bit in a pan the evening before the bread-making; as each panful was mixed to her satisfaction it was handed over to the other women present to add to the mass of dough they had started to tread, wrapped in a cloth, or *savan*, of linen thread woven ages ago in a herringbone pattern. The cloth had to be strong, for when Gülazar had finished adding her panfuls to it there must have been two or three hundredweight of tough dough there, and it was being heavily trodden by five or six women, myself among them. Once it had been flattened, it was rolled up both ways into a round hill, still in the cloth, and trodden out again. We had clean bare feet but it was forbidden to let a foot touch the dough. After an hour or two it was judged fit to leave for the night. At dawn it was hacked into hunks of identical weight with a huge knife, then rolled and, as it were, tucked by its outer skin into smooth round balls, the size of croquet balls. Then representatives of the five households sat round, each woman at her own short-legged bread-board, sticking her feet out underneath it, so that one saw bare feet or patched socks in front of each board. With a rolling-pin more than a metre long and about two centimetres thick, each ball of dough was rolled out until it was a metre wide and very very thin, so as to be translucent if not transparent. Then, hanging half on each side of the rolling-pin, it was passed to the cook, who unrolled it with one swift sure movement on to the hot iron over the firepit. After a moment it was lifted with the long rolling-pin and put down again on the hot iron to brown on the other side. Then it was lifted off, put on a pile beside the cook, and another sheet of dough hanging on its rolling-pin was taken up and smoothly put on the iron. As the heap of cooked bread mounted it was lifted by another of the women and taken and put on the top of the pile in the storeroom.

All that was serious work, but when the women were hungry, or some children came back from school, dough would be rolled out to a width of eighteen inches, much thicker than the *yufka* bread, and spread with the yolk and white of an egg, some broken cheese, some butter, and lots of fresh parsley. Then it was folded in two and cooked on the iron. They all loved that cheese bread; it was very rich. They rolled it up and ate it at once.

The fire pit is called a *tandır*, it goes down about a metre into the ground and is usually bordered with stones or cement, but it is always a danger to toddlers. There is a brick pipe going into the side of it to provide air, and any old dry twigs and leaves are burnt in it. Beans are put in earthenware pots and cooked in the ashes after the bread-making; jacket potatoes are baked in the ashes too. Everyday meals are cooked at a small hearth between stones in the same great cave room that contains the *tandır*. The cave interior is of a round beehive shape with two openings in the top through which sunlight streams; all round it are little shelves and nooks and niches in the rock, where oddments are stored, such things as no farm wife wants to throw away.

The bread-boards are lovely things, in one piece, top and legs, of beech nowadays, which will last twenty years, but Harun's mother had one of dark walnut, and walnut will last for fifty years. Loaf bread is not eaten much in the village houses, but the thin unleavened *yufka*, made always to the recipe I gave above, is moistened and wrapped in a cloth for half an hour before a meal, to soften it, and a handful is set on the tablecloth at each place.

Bulgur is made from wheat and used in the village for pilau, instead of expensive rice brought from the south. A girl stands in the willow shade by the stream; blue woodsmoke eddies round her as she stirs a wide pan. I cross by the wooden footbridge and ask what she is cooking.

'I'm cooking *bulgur*, come back in two hours and eat some.'

It was good: hot porridge which needed neither milk nor sugar to make it palatable. For true *bulgur*, the cooked wheat would be dried and then broken small in a mill. Our people use the mill under a small mosque in our quarter; a vertical stone wheel, a bit like a Hereford cider mill, revolves on a round platform, the wheat is kept in its path, and in an hour a sackful may be broken small. The wide basalt wheel has a tree trunk fixed to it by which it is turned; the motive power can be a donkey or, if none is available, a couple of women. The wheel revolves slowly, I marked it and it goes round once for two circlings of the donkey. The name for the stone wheel is *dink*.

Like other wheat-processing gear, it is ancient. One day I saw a woman grinding *bulgur* in a black basalt hand-quern. I asked where it came from.

'Oh, it's always been in our family.'

Probably, but if it were in a museum it would be labelled Bronze Age.

3. Gülten at the door to the roof

4. The Meydan
   in winter

4

WOMEN AT WORK

The grape harvest is not so profoundly important to village life as the wheat harvest, though it is spread over a longer period, and in cash terms it is, or could be, worth more. The volcanic soil is what the vine likes. The vineyards are all over the steppe-like plateau lands and on the valley slopes. Many kinds of grapes are grown, ripening at different times between July and October. All the family holdings are fragmented, that is they are scattered all over the village lands. This is due to the system of inheritance; each child inherits equally. Everything possible is done to group holdings together by territorial marriages, often between first cousins, or by buying in family land if the inheritor wishes to sell. But fragmented holdings are a problem all over Turkey and hold back the modernization of agricultural methods.

Every small area of the village lands has its name, like the field names on English farms. Moonmouth, the Top of the Frying-pan, the Secret Place, the Church Vineyard, the Open Palace, the Cold Spring. At Tortoise Spring Vineyard, steps lead down into the earth to a dark pool of good water. Haci Baba had contracted to sell nearly two tons of grapes from that vineyard to the wine factory. Boxes had been brought out by tractor and trailer and stacked at the ends of the rows. Haci Baba's eldest daughter's lad was there, big, handsome, soon to do his military service, called Mehmet; also his sister, rather plain then but very reliable and with a splendid readiness to laugh—I liked her very much. The vineyard was in a hot hollow surrounded by oleaster bushes bent down with the weight of their yellow date-like fruit. The work went well, the vines were heavy with fruit of a perfect degree of ripeness, and we kept running down to the ends of the rows with full buckets to empty them into the boxes; each bunch must be held carefully in the left hand, the stalk is cut with a saw-edged knife in the right hand, then the cut bunch is placed in the bucket. Melon plants between the vines bore ripe fruit for us to eat at rest time. Here and there hemp plants grew tall; their seeds would be dried for nibbling at winter parties.

Apple and peach trees grew between the vines too, to provide fruit for the family; some peach trees bear heavy crops of small delicious golden fruit. The children told me it was *haram* to eat anyone else's peaches; a very strong word they also employed to tell me that it was forbidden to eat pig meat. The peaches are very good; anyone may eat a handful of someone else's grapes if they are hungry or thirsty, so it must have been especially impressed on the children that the peaches were not to be touched. They are a marginal crop in Nar because of the late frosts, but those little peaches often escape when the frost has nipped all the apricot bloom. Olives cannot grow there at all because of the cold winters.

When all the grape boxes were full, and the required tonnage had been totted up, we sat in the shade and ate a meal while we waited for transport to come from the wine factory. Kazim cut a dry sunflower stalk and made a popgun for his little son, Mehmet. The trigger was made from a springy twig and the missile from a smaller piece of dry stalk. Mediha, the laughter-prone cousin, found a tiny lizard like a jewel where she was doing her *namaz*, and she brought it for us all to admire.

Some of the grape-juice is pasteurized and sold as a cool drink; some is fermented into wine. Haci Baba is a God-fearing man who has a big family to provide for; there is a conflict in his mind between the suitability of the soil for grapes and the fact that alcohol is forbidden to Muslims.

Harun's mother had one or two vineyards, but her family lived in the town and all of them had salaried jobs. One of their vineyards had run wild, asphodel and iris grew under the poplars; she rented it to someone who cleared the flowers and planted wheat. From another vineyard she picked as much as the family wanted, sending basketfuls to Harun in Ankara, and then late in the year picked the remaining grapes for the wine factory. We set out with an old woman and a donkey to pick the fruit which had mostly dried and turned into raisins through being left till October. The old woman with the donkey knew all the varieties. There were some long black ones, like the green finger grapes but thinly spaced in the bunch, that she ate with enjoyment; she said they were called Goats' Teats. When we had finished picking and were waiting for the boy to fetch a van to take the fruit to the factory she sat down with a bunch of small round pinky-yellow grapes. She looked up laughing and said they were called Cock's Balls, they were her favourite but not planted any more. All names are not so countrified; Cloud grapes are planted in new vineyards and they are beautiful to look at, a grey cloud colour. The best liked are the huge round Sergeant grapes, a light greenish colour with few seeds. There are the big black Antep grapes, and the Muscat, and the despised late black Kayseri ones that make gigantic vines.

The ordinary white grapes are boiled down in October for the sugar syrup or *pekmez*, which until twenty years ago was the only sugar the villagers ever saw. It is hot and burning to the mouth, a brown syrup. The grapes are trodden in big vats as they used to be in Early Christian times for wine; you can see the old wine-treading arrangements here and there in caves, with crosses cut in the walls to show that the juice was holy. The villagers wash their feet three times with soap before they tread the grapes, and shuffle backwards and forwards over them for an hour or two. Next day they are trodden again and that second run of juice is put aside unboiled to become vinegar, used for making pickles. The first treading of the grapes produces the juice which is boiled in big copper pans; then calcium carbonate from a mine north of the big river is added to clear it; then it is strained and boiled again to syrup. It is used in various forms—a sort of Turkish delight is a popular sweet; for this it is thickened with wheat starch. Bees are kept but the honey can be sold for such a high price that it is a luxury; it is given to ill people as a cure-all. Factory beet sugar is obtainable from any village shop today.

That year Haci Baba was going to dry the grapes in a vineyard down the Gülşehir road, overlooking the valley of the Kızıl Irmak. It was an old vineyard and the stocks were tall, though of course they had been pruned back to almost nothing every March; they were bearing very heavily too. If vines are regularly attended to, pruned and dug around and manured and dusted with sulphur in summer, they go on bearing more and more heavily. Haci Baba's eldest daughter and her husband were there that day, with their daughter Mediha. They had a cart with a white horse; ours was black. He had no name, horses practically never do, they called him *Beygir*, stallion, but all the horses in Nar are that, and all the asses jackasses. They are bred in herds in mountain villages and our men buy them at market and often train them themselves. That stallion was old, and they sold him in the winter and bought a woolly brown one they call *Tay*, the colt.

At first we picked the raisin grapes quickly in the freshness of the summer morning, laying them to dry on long ramps which Kazim shaped and flattened with a shovel. We'd finished by noon and went back to the son-in-law's vineyard at the corner of the track to the Cold Spring. By then the day was very hot and there was no shade there even for the horses. We picked on with steady determination; they begged me to rest; I replied that they were tired too, wanted a rest just as much as I. I went on sharing the work. When you are tired it is very easy to waste grapes, to cut the bunches clumsily without cupping them in your left hand, so that grapes are scattered on the earth; Haci Baba insisted that they must all be picked up—to leave them was scorning God's bounty. No question of man hours, or woman hours, entered into it. We got tired indeed. I lay flat on the nubbly earth and said how lovely tea would be; the owner of the vineyard, Haci Baba's son-in-law, sent me over a bunch of round green Sergeant grapes the size of ping-pong balls, saying they were tea. We worked on like sleepwalkers till there was only one row left and he said he'd do that easily next day. Goodness knows how we climbed into the cart and went home to a meal and bed. Next morning I woke and saw the basket of pink grapes they had given me standing proudly in the middle of my whitewashed room.

The cut grapes in the vineyard would be dried for a week on one side and then someone would go out and turn all the bunches over to be dried for a week on the other. They'd be taken home in sacks and sold as required, after the women had picked all the dry brown stems off. In fact, the cash for the grape crop depends on the labour of the women; it is pleasant work, done in company, often in the street where three women will gather by a sunny doorway to clean grapes. They can't read or write and they enjoy working with each other and seeing the passers-by. That's the way things are in Nar.

Walnut gathering happens about the end of September. Around the middle of August the walnut groves, each containing two or three big trees, are irrigated to plump and fill the nuts. All the plots have irrigation channels that water can be turned into by a girl with a shovel. Later in the autumn, when the shells are hard inside their green cases, the gathering is planned for what is looked forward to as a happy day; the chance for a picnic, and company, and a change from routine. A young and able-bodied man is the key worker; he climbs the tree carrying a heavy ten-foot pole and beats the branches till all the walnuts have fallen. The women and children pick them up from the ground, and in our family, prudent granny gathers all the fallen green leaves and pushes them into sacks for stockfeed.

Down at Fatma Bağ, by the stream, Kazim was in and out of view up in the treetop, like a grey gorilla, steadying himself as he swung the pole. The girls and his second wife and I collected nuts from the green damp grass under the trees and from the stream. That was really fun; they'd come down the fast current sometimes in bunches, sometimes singly, and we'd field them laughing and throw them into a bucket. The walnuts from Fatma Bağ would fill four or five sacks. They get perhaps seventy lira a thousand for them, roughly the equivalent of two pounds sterling; quite a useful amount of money. A thousand walnuts makes about half a sack. Then Gülten, the eldest girl, lit a fire and roasted some aubergines till they were black and burnt outside; she peeled them and we ate the tender green inner flesh rolled inside thin bread, with or without white cheese. Quince bushes were all round us but the brown-furred fruit ripens late and it was too hard to bite. The tomatoes and watermelons in the gardens by the walnut grove were ripe and we had plenty of those.

The walnuts are dried on the roof for a day or two and the green cases removed, an absolutely filthy job. The women do not worry about rubber gloves and their hands, especially their fingernails, get quite black. The walnut cases are saved to dye the wool they spin for socks and cardigans. Then the bare nuts must be dried for another day

or two; when fresh, the yellow leathery skin covering the white
flesh is very bitter; it only becomes papery and tasteless when the nuts
are fully dry. Nar walnuts then have a creamy coloured inner skin;
Istanbul walnuts have a less attractive brown one.

Turks have an amazing gift for the most delightful and memorable
picnics. A teacher's family strolling down towards a walnut grove one
Sunday took me with them and spread rugs on the ground and made
tea. Sabiha and Nurcan, the teenage daughters, Chinese-looking and
dressed with quiet charm, who came to look for flowers with me,
could not believe that the obsidian tools scattered on the hillside had
been chipped by men thousands of years ago. Huriye, their mother,
was utterly good and calm, and extended her motherliness to me; I
was so much at peace in her presence that I lay and sank blissfully into
sleep in the light shade under the walnut trees. Some women friends
came along and sat waiting for me to wake up so that we could all
walk to the top of the valley where there is a lovely waterfall. They told
me that the narrow and tree-filled valley just below the falls was called
Kadirak, but it meant nothing to them, merely a place name. To me it
was a reminder of the former Greek inhabitants. Ikbal Hanım, Harun's
mother, organized another picnic at Uzengi Wadi, the Stirrup Valley,
overhung by high rose-coloured cliffs full of pigeon caves. We sat by
a stream which flowed between apple trees laden with fruit; a blue-
winged bee-eater had worn the top twig of a tree bare and he sat
waiting for a fly or a bee to pass by, when he would swoop joyfully
on it. Ikbal Hanım did her *namaz* ritual in that lovely place; when she
had done we walked up beside the water and gathered armfuls of blue
globe thistles and filled our cans with the naturally bubbly mineral
water from a spring.

The women do most of the work in the vegetable gardens. If men
are available they may do the heavy digging, but the women are responsible for the planting and weeding and harvesting. One April day
on a garden plot near the Fatma Bağ walnut grove I watched Kazim's
two wives planting onion sets. They sat themselves down in their
dust-coloured *dimi* and stuck the tiny onions well into the ground in
front of them, advancing over the plot on their haunches and firming
the sets in their earth with their well-clothed bottoms. That day was

54

very warm; summer had come and at lunchtime we sat in the sun eating a salad of the pink petals of quince flowers the girls had collected. April weather was not always so mild; I went for a walk down the valley when a ferocious north-easterly wind was blowing, thickening the air with a choking fog of dust and making the tall poplars wave to and fro like metronomes, so that their branches rubbed together with unearthly shrieks and groans. Three women strange to me were busy planting onion sets in a tiny hillside plot. One stood with her legs straddled boldly, a caricature of a primitive peasant, chewing an end of raw cabbage. The bare skin of her feet was dry and wrinkled like that of an animal. The women asked me most politely to visit them in their houses; I knew if I managed to accept their invitation they would receive me with gracious formality and offer me coffee in delicate newly-washed cups on a fine tray, like great ladies in the Sultan's harem. Yet a village woman's pride in making the earth bring forth food is almost as great as her pride in being the mother of sons.

Her house is probably bare of furniture by our standards; the senior women have rooms furnished only with carpets and cushions on floor and window-seat. Modern brides like to have four armchairs, a settee, a buffet, and so on. In all houses, small treasures which might get dusty or be admired by a guest (I had to learn never to admire anything or it would be offered me as a gift) are put away. Everything is swept with a short broom and dusted every day. Twice a year, for the two great festivals, the Sugar Festival and the Sacrifice Festival, the house and everything in it must be thoroughly washed. The house is then fitted up with the best cushions and carpets from the store-room, and the freshly-bathed family put on new dresses and suits to sit at home with *ikram*, guest dishes, ready for guests, or they go visiting themselves. The festivals are the time for visiting; if you are walking to see someone, or travelling by bus or car to do so, you are a *bayramci*, a festivaller.

While I was there the festivals fell during the winter months, they move round the western or solar year because of the religious lunar calendar. They were very pleasant, but even without them, the cold months are not idle ones; all the dresses have to be made, and the wool which will be knitted into socks, warm vests and cardigans has to be spun. Wool also has to be washed and teased out and stuffed into mattress covers, a duty which fell heavily on our household, for we had four girls and each must have four sets of bedding when she marries. A girl's bottom drawer is thought of, and her household things are got together from the time she is born. Material value is given for the high brideprice sometimes asked.

Childbirth occurs with no fuss and no publicity. There is a State-trained midwife in Nar and within call in every village, but she isn't always summoned. People cling to old ways. Our midwife, like all those I met, was a serious and conscientious girl devoted to the well-being of those under her care. Unfortunately congenital dislocation of the hip is not uncommon in the villages, and people, finding a child unable to walk at the right age, put the misplaced bone down to a too vigorous shaking by the midwife, in her efforts to make the infant yell and breathe. The young girls are certainly frightened that the babies won't start breathing, but whatever the cause of the dislocation, it isn't their shaking.

I met two young midwives in the house of a most respected widow, who maintained gently that the old-fashioned birth position had something to be said for it, squatting on the floor with a friend on each side of you to support you and another to receive and care for the baby. The girls said they were taught that it was better to get the mother on to a bed, where the progress of the birth could be carefully watched.

One day my good friend Münüre Höke, usually a cheery woman, came to my door with her face distorted by worry and distress.

'Oh God,' she said, 'my daughter-in-law is about to do a birth, she is very bad, it is much sooner than we thought. Can you take her to hospital?'

That was when I had a VW Beetle.

'I can take my car up to Salim Hoca's mosque and turn it as soon as you can get Seher there,' I said. 'Let's go.' I picked them up; Münüre got into the back andstarted praying, Seher sat beside me, gripping the hand-rail, her face bent within her shawl, tense, bravely silent. I was praying too, but we got up the hill into the hospital and I jumped out.

The porter was seated behind his grand desk, surrounded by a crowd of applicants for treatment, with all their relatives.

'I come from Nar, my neighbour is about to give birth, she is just there outside in my car. Where can we take her to see a doctor or midwife?'

The porter, flattered in his male vanity at having an English-woman to talk to in front of that crowd, uncrossed his legs, leaned forward, looked soulfully up into my eyes and said:

'The Doctor, oh he's having his midday meal, he's gone, he may be here this afternoon, I don't know where the midwife is.'

'Look you', I said, 'get going. My neighbour is about to have a baby in my car there. Where is she to go?'

He awoke to the situation; we followed him, helping Seher, to the midwife's office, where the midwife arrived as soon as Seher's *dimi* were off.

One look.

'You've got five minutes. Don't put your *dimi* on again. Follow me to the ward.'

In a quarter of an hour I looked down on Seher smiling at her lovely boy. He was to be called Nütfü. Her first son, after two girls. Münüre was dazed and quiet with joy beside the bed. Seher was bored in hospital and came home in two days. The following week Münüre asked me to take her husband Osman, herself, Seher and the baby to see Seher's parents at the village of Avcilar, fifteen kilometres to the east. It was to be an evening visit; I waited for them to come back from the fields and wash and tidy themselves. Then at first they said Seher and the babe were not coming.

'Why? I want specially to take them, she will be so proud.'

'The navel cord has not yet dropped off,' said Münüre. 'It is not good manners to visit another house until it has.'

'But it is her own house. Please let her come.'

They relented. Münüre marched into the Avcilar house with the babe held out across both arms in front of her.

'The cord hasn't fallen off. Forgive us.' Honest of her, how would they know? The babe was well swaddled.

It was not a rich house, all was bare and simple. It was a ceremonial visit and formality took over, the presentation of the Lady Seher who had given her husband's family a manchild, the gracious raising of Seher to a position of honour in her husband's family. We sat together speaking quietly for two hours; first tea and then coffee was brought to us on trays with fresh lace cloths, and a tinned copper tray piled with the best of their grapes was always beside us. Everyone was deeply happy. I was too, for Seher has a gift for bringing up her babies to smile; the two little girls have most memorable smiles.

5

CEREMONIES

The circumcision of a little son or the marriage of a son or daughter are occasions for hospitality and celebration in every family.

I don't like having to write about circumcision because it is cruel, but it plays an important part in a boy's life. A proud grandfather will look forward for years to the grand circumcision party he will give for his grandson. It is the pride of boys in enduring the pain stoically which has ensured the continuance of the rite as part of modern Turkish life. Does the shared endurance add to the undoubted brotherhood between all Muslims? I was lucky to be taken to my first circumcision party by a girl whom I respected deeply, a biology student at Hacettepe Medical University at Ankara. Münevver and her younger sister lived with their mother, a cousin of Seher's father-in-law, in Nar. Her father had been a building contractor, whose chief pride was a fine school, and her much older brother was the X-ray specialist at Kayseri Hospital. Münevver had heard that I was living in Nar. English is very important, almost the teaching language, at Hacettepe, and Münevver came to ask me for help in conversation practice. She was thoughtful and intelligent and I was glad to give her all the help I could.

I went with her and her sister to their apple orchard down the valley; they had their donkey with them and I rode him down through the rippling shallows of the stream while the girls ran along the bank. In the orchard we picked up the windfalls and loaded them into the panniers, cut some clover and turned what had been cut a day or two before. Nightingales sang and hoopoes flew their swerving flights between the trees. I told Münevver about the book I hoped to write and she told me how she had really wanted to do pharmacy but her father's illness during her final exams at Lycée had worried her and she hadn't done as well as she could have. She was working hard at biology so that if there should be a vacancy in the pharmacy course they would let her transfer to it.

It was a day or two later when she asked me to go with her to the circumcision party; her neighbour's two boys and another child were being circumcised. They were aged from six to nine. At nine o'clock one morning we went in and sat with thirty well-dressed women in a stuffy sitting-room. The three boys in white suits with embroidered caps on their heads came round and kissed our hands, touching them to their foreheads. The boys with all their guests got into some decorated taxis and went for a drive to the cemetery in the town, where we went to their grandfather's grave and knelt and prayed with the nervous children.

Back at home a white bed had been prepared with embroidered cushions. Münevver and I stood in the hall. We heard shrill screams. I was determined to behave properly and with respect for their customs; looking through the open door of the bedroom I saw a photographer standing on the bottom rail of the bed trying to get a good view. Six men in tweed caps were holding a child down. Presently one or two stood aside to give us a good view. The Health Officer was powdering the boy's genitals and bloody cotton wool had been thrown into a polythene bowl. A long blue robe was put on the little boy and his father picked him up and took him out to the balcony in his arms to show him to the men in the street.

The next boy was done, and the last started.

'Put your headscarf on so as to cover all your hair,' said Münevver. 'Salim Hoca is going to read the *Mevlud*, a poem about the birth of our Prophet, it takes about an hour.'

'I don't like this, Münevver,' I said.

'I don't either, but our Prophet said it was a good custom.'

One afternoon when I had been feeling ill with a temperature from some bug or other Gülazar and Nazmiye insisted on taking me to what they said was a party in the town to cheer me up. When we arrived I found that three great-grandchildren of Haci Nazmiye were being circumcised, the eldest perhaps twelve, the youngest a baby.

We opened the door on a very loud noise, two fiddlers scraping away as loudly as they could in a hopeless effort to drown the yells of a twelve-year-old boy. Men were holding him down with his bare legs apart over a big polythene washing-up bowl. An old grey un-shaven drunken gipsy man was sawing away at his foreskin, every now and then refreshing himself with a swig from a bottle of *raki* from which he drank while still squatting, raising it to his mouth after he had transferred the knife to his left hand.

I went into the next room which I was glad to find empty and began to cry. I was ashamed of myself but in fact I wasn't well. The boy's mother and father came and held my hands; they looked unhappy too. It wasn't so much the boy's agony that worried me, though his parents thought it was, it was breaking their own hearts, but the shining eyes of the old men and women watching, delighting lasciviously in the cruelty. How low can the human race go?

They did the three boys and put them into beds. As we were leaving we saw the father's face go white; he had lifted the bedclothes from the oldest boy to see that he was literally lying in a pool of blood; he wasn't asleep as had been thought but in a coma. We left them to it, they didn't want us.

The boy recovered and was getting about in three days. I was told that boys who die while they are being circumcised go straight to Paradise.

That last occasion was what they call a comic circumcision; people throw the musicians money and they are paid only a small sum, if at all, by the parents. It is only a few lira anyhow . . . why do they do it? People in Nar preferred to use the Health Officer, Osman Effendi.

I hated circumcisions for their indecency and cruelty. Weddings were a different matter and I found them absorbingly interesting even when I didn't, as at first, know the girl who was being married.

Münevver and her sister had a family of cousins, Memnune, her sisters and their mother Meliha, born Höke, now Yilmaz who took me to a traditional village wedding at Ortahisar, Middle Castle, so called from a towering rock in the middle of the little town, a rock which had been cut out and hollowed into a fortress a hundred feet high.

The Yilmaz family were particularly interesting to me because they illustrated the partial migration to Germany which is eroding the old independent village life. A man can earn in Germany ten times what he can in Turkey, and so can women; there is of course very very little paid work available to women in Turkey. If wives go with their husbands they like it there and adapt very quickly to being good *hausfraus*, doing the household shopping every morning. (Shopping is a man's job in Turkey.) They can earn good wages too, and girls can go to technical school and learn German well enough to be employed as interpreters in the factories. They have told me often how clean Germany is, and what lovely gardens their houses there have; Turkish women look slim and western when they get out of the habit of putting on baggy old *dimi* every time they go out. But they always think of their Turkish village, with its close, warm friendships, as home.

The family I am telling you about, the Yilmaz family whose mother was first cousin to Münevver's mother, were having a big picnic in the woods and they asked me to go with them. I was told by the girls that it was to be a goodbye picnic, their mother and Memnune, the eldest daughter, were going back to Germany with their father in his Opel car.

Meliha, the mother, a handsome youngish woman, was sitting sewing while her male relations, brothers and father, talked on a rug a little way away. Memnune too sat sewing, her head bent. Children played around and three donkeys were tied up, donkeys which had been loaded with pots of food. The father I saw along a woodland avenue talking to an old man who was hoeing his marrows. The children took me round and showed me a spring and an irrigation tank.

Two days later the youngest girl came to my door early in the morning.

'My dad's gone . . .', glumly.

'Oh . . . hasn't your mother gone with him?'

'No, she's lying ill.'

I went round to their house and found the mother in a coma of weeping, careless of my presence, her swollen face half-covered by the quilt. Her father and brother had in effect prevented her going to

Germany by flatly refusing to look after any of her five children. By completely giving way to her grief she was able to get through it, and to go on with her life in a day or two, cheerfully and without bitterness.

It was a month after that that they took me to the wedding in Ortahisar. I went with two of the girls, who led me to a door in a wall in the strange village, and through it into the guest room, where we were welcomed, I by an old lady who was blind and deaf but who maintained touch by warm kissing.

The house was entirely given over to the women wedding guests, the men were elsewhere. Mealtimes were astonishing, with thirty women sitting round a big, low table-board on the floor. On my right was a lovely red-head with big green eyes and a pre-Raphaelite face, whose baby, a few weeks old, was on the floor behind her. A woman of the family with a glowing, peachy face brought a vast blue enamel bowl of soup and, bending over, set it in the middle of the round board. It had to be in the middle so that all could stretch their spoons to get an equal share. Other dishes followed, with rice pudding and an almondy semolina dish in the middle, then meat, beans and another savoury dish again. After the meal we watched a team of gipsy dancers out in the court under a green vine. The chief dance was a very good *köçek*, always done by gipsy entertainers. The dancer wore a completely circular red silk skirt, which stood out horizontally as he spun round and round, clicking the iron castanets attached to his fingers. He twitched his stomach and twisted his head to one side with a game-cock-like fierceness. A red cummerbund was twisted round his hips to accentuate their movements. A fiddler and a *darbuka* player accompanied him; the *darbuka* is a narrow, small-waisted drum. The dancer kept strictly to the strong beat even when he bent over backwards to pick up a five-lira note with his teeth.

The bride, a quiet thin child of sixteen, was trying on dresses and having her hair done in a guestroom. When I asked where the bride-groom was a little boy volunteered to take me through the village to see him, on the other side of the quarter. On our way there we went to a big vaulted room where all the men guests were assembled, sitting cross-legged on cushions down the sides of the room. The musicians were at the far end. I smoked a cigarette and ate two sweets sitting beside a polite gentleman, but a woman was an embarrassment there, though children of both sexes romped in and out unrebuked. We went on to find the bridegroom sitting with a young man friend in a room bare of furnishings, with fresh green paintwork. The bridegroom said his name was Mehmet and his job was driving a delivery van round the Kayseri district; he was eighteen so there were two years before he would be liable for military service. 'Oh, I know my bride well, I've loved her for a year,' he told me. I expect he meant he had seen her in the distance and greeted her in her father's house once. The room where we were talking would be their nuptial chamber, the only place where they might ever speak to each other; it opened off the court of his father's house.

I walked around the village and that afternoon found him being shaved on a *kilim* spread in the street, while pipes and drum played. A boy brought a pair of shiny black shoes, held out as though they were the crown at a coronation, then another came with a new suit on a hanger, then another with a folded pile on top of which was a shirt. His friends closed round the bridegroom and began to dress him, while I went back to the women's house to see the bride.

She was being prepared too. Her hair was being piled up in the high, rolled coiffure brides like, with a long lock hanging down over one shoulder. (Once married, a woman's hair has always to be covered, even at night when she wraps it in a white muslin cloth.) The rolls of hair did not suit her long, thin face and she looked peaky and withdrawn. Several new dresses hung on the wall, presents from the bridegroom. She would show herself in each of them in turn, changing every few hours and emerging again before all the women.

When a long tail of silver tinsel and a crown of white cotton flowers had been added to her headdress the whole thing was topped with a thin, red silk veil covered with sequins in a pattern of the sun and stars. Brides must always wear something red; I asked why and was told it was because red was the colour of the Turkish flag; truly I think it symbolizes her virginity. Common red field poppies are called Little Brides . . . *Gelincik.*

We left her finishing her toilet and went to dance in the shade of a mulberry tree at the top of the hill, where there was a cool movement of air; the day was becoming very hot, Ortahisar is in a hollow like an oven. A woman with a hare-lip was playing the *def*, a big tambourine covered with the stretched skin of a cow's stomach. It is an instrument peculiar to women and is always used for women to dance to at weddings. Some of the women had as many as forty gold medallions hung round their necks, five hundred pounds worth of inflation-proof jewellery clanking richly as they moved.

The warmth and the golden light made an idyllic setting. Each woman showed her personality in the way she danced: a tall girl in brown print, her face calm against the shimmering leaves, her eyelids sky-blue with eye shadow, swayed clicking her fingers; a fat Arab-type beauty clicked her fingers at shoulder level and revolved slowly, her intense concentration, her broad face and the upturned corners of her mouth making her look like a carved *apsara* from an Indian cave; a girl with a dimpled chin and long plaits moved her belly erotically; another had green eyes tilted up at the corners and was self-conscious, aware of our eyes on her, playing up.

I could have watched the dancing for hours, it was extremely pleasant, but little boys climbing up the mulberry tree to get a better view sent showers of dust and bits of bark all over me and the dust stuck to my sweating skin; glancing at the girls I had come with I told them I wanted to see what was going on back in the house.

Another meal was being prepared; that evening they were going to feed the women in three sessions. They were cooking on an open hearth and also on a little fireplace set in the wall, which they called a *şemine*, cheminée. They set the bread to rise in small round loaves, having mixed the dough with a small amount of old dough to act as yeast. They didn't make flat *yufka* bread in Ortahisar.

After two sittings had eaten supper, the *defci* with the scarred mouth began to play in the yard; we all sat close together, very sweaty and sticky. I was glad when the bride and my young friends suggested we should go and watch the men dancing in the street.

In the wide space at the bottom the men were wheeling in the dance called a *halay*. The man at the inside end kicked away in one place while all the other dancers in line wheeled, pivoting on him. The outside two swung to the ground at every step, sweeping handkerchiefs around in the air. Next, two men danced opposite each other like two birds displaying in a courtship ritual. Another *halay* made me think of hunters celebrating a capture, treading out a circle. I saw Mehmet the bridegroom among the dancers. The women stood huddled in a corner like huge white moths, hidden under their all-enveloping sheets. I'm sure Mehmet couldn't have distinguished the bride among them. Pipe and drum banged out the rhythm.

Back at the house the henna had to be put on, it was Wednesday, the henna night. A village wedding starts on Monday, Wednesday is henna night, the bride is taken to the new house on the Thursday, and the wedding finishes with a feast in the bridegroom's house on the Friday.

One of the women had mixed the greeny-brown henna powder with enough water to make a thick paste in a bowl; the bride came out and sat on a chair to have it applied. She was wearing long pyjama trousers and a nightdress of flowered flannelette. The paste was put on the palm of a hand, then that was wrapped in paper, then in rags, and an embroidered mitt slipped over it all. The process was repeated with the other hand. It was done carefully and took about twenty minutes. It didn't take so long to do her toes, wrap them in rags, and push them into loose sandals. Most of the women put henna in the palm of their right hand and wrapped a rag round the clenched fist for the night, so that the colour had time to take on the skin. Henna is only put in the palm but it stains the finger-joints and nails too. The nails turn a dark colour and stay that way until it grows out at the tip, but the colour on the skin is paler and wears off in a week or two. They said the Prophet liked women to henna their hands and feet and hair.

There were babies asleep in one of the rooms, and when our mattresses and quilts were laid out in the big cave room where the bride was sleeping the mothers collected their children to sleep with them. They were well-behaved in a strange house, I hardly heard a sound all night, and the wool mattresses and quilts were cosy to sleep in. The men I suppose slept in another house. The bride lay next to the window under a pink silk quilt with a special friend on each side of her. She had begun to come to life, to smile a little, when the henna was on; her wedding was next day.

In what seemed no time I was woken by drumming, getting louder and louder. I sat up; someone opened the door and I could look out at the dark yard. The morning call to prayer had been read but I had not heard it, and outside I saw the bridegroom and his friends dancing under the vine to the sound of flute and drum; they had come to awaken the bride.

Two women helped her to her feet and stood beside her supporting her, all of them draped in sheets. Mehmet was there dancing for his bride, who looked like Aphrodite risen from the sea, flanked by her two attendants. The electric light in the yard was on and it shone through the green vineleaves; the women were silhouetted against it. The sky paled and, with a burst of festive gunfire, the men were gone.

Soon the women got up and put the breakfast bread outside to rise in the warmth of the newly risen sun. We undid our hands and feet to see how the henna had taken. The bride's toes were a very fine bright orange.

The dowry with all its embroideries was laid out for our inspection in a side room. I was admiring them and wondering how many woman-hours had been put into the work, when I heard a groan in a dark corner and found the bride's mother sobbing helplessly. It is the custom for the bride's mother to give way weeping. She is losing a dear companion who has grown into her ways, whose body and character she has formed.

Outside in the sunny lane, all the men were wondering how many donkeys would be needed to take the gear to the new house. Soon the mother stopped crying for a time and the men started bringing all the things out and sorting them into donkey-size piles. Loud arguments occurred about three big awkward wooden chests. There were carpets and cushions and mattresses of all shapes and colours. I was told that for this particular wedding the bride's father had bought all these things; the groom's father had given the bride fifteen gold medallions and her dresses. I should hate to have my outfits chosen by someone else, who didn't even know me very well, but it is the custom. I can, however, see a certain beauty in the groom's purchase of the wedding dress.

The wedding was to be legally registered at once, that very day. Though they looked young the bride was sixteen and the groom eighteen. If the couple is below the legal age, they tie the religious knot and have the dancing, and leave the civil registration until they are old enough. Girls in many villages beg their parents to find them a husband as soon as they are thirteen. Women consider the dancing the binding part of a wedding; the hocas or priests, the religious bond; the Government, the registration. I have never had the chance of seeing the religious bond tied.

The time had come to dress the bride for the registration at the municipal offices. They put on a pink brocade dress, knee-length, the complete white crown and veil headdress, nylon stockings and brown, patent leather shoes. She might well have been a bride in a small English village, except that she wasn't smiling radiantly and making everyone happy to look at her. She looked serious, but all the same there was something, that shy bony little face had a certain charm. It must be wonderful to be awakened by one's bridegroom dancing for one; the shock of it really happening to her had indeed awakened her.

The next part was dreadful; they veiled her in shabby rusty black, her face and her legs and everything, except the brown patent shoes. They said the men must not look at her; any male look is assumed to be one of lust for someone else's property. Then she was dragged downhill and up again to the offices on the square, those patent shoes twinkling helplessly; poor thing, she couldn't see the rough ground and the steps through the thick veil. Oh, it was all very proper, no doubt, to them.

The women all tumbled up the office steps together, pushing and scrambling and getting in each other's way, frightened as rabbits to be out in the open. At last we were crowded into the back of the dusty office which no woman was ever allowed to clean. The couple were seated at one end of a big polished table, the bride very awkwardly, straddling the corner of her chair, her knees well apart. They signed a book. The marriage registrar sat at the far end of the table and other men sat at its sides. For what seemed a very long time we women stood at the back of the room while the numerous children scuttered about with a total lack of ceremony or respect for the solemn occasion. Nothing happened. We all (except the children) kept still and silent while a patch of sunlight falling on the table moved about a foot.

At last a man moved. Sweets and cigarettes were handed round, and we could go. The women found their own shoes on the dusty landing and went home in small knots, poking the sweets under their veils and into their mouths. They rushed in through the yard door as soon as they got there, glad to have reached sanctuary.

I stood outside watching the last things put on the donkeys, six of which had been found necessary. I asked one of the Yilmaz girls standing beside me if she ever thought at all of her own marriage; she blushed deeply and said her older sister would have to be married first. When the donkeys were loaded they set off to the nuptial chamber; we went there by a quicker way, a short cut through the close-packed houses using steps and back yards.

The little bare room was full of women all having a good time and getting in each other's way. They were determined to make the room as lovely as they possibly could but each had different ideas about what should go where. Bundles from the donkeys were poked in through the window and children were literally underfoot. The women were curious about the contents of the big chests and pulled things out; each had seen some particular piece of embroidery she planned to put somewhere, and of course the required piece was always at the bottom. After half an hour, the bed was piled with a neat arrangement of silk quilts and cushions and hung with embroidered side curtains. A girl with her own ideas had borrowed an adze from the people in the yard outside and was hammering nails into the wall with the back of it to hang up the gaudiest of the carpets. Then someone put a row of copper pots on the shelf over the window and the remaining cushions were put over the floor like very plump tiles.

A man shouted from outside:

'Oh God. Allah Allah, haven't you finished yet? You in there? Hurry up, do, the bride is coming . . . here she comes.'

Everyone tidied the bit round her own feet and we all went out into the yard, shooing the children before us. Some kind lady made me stand pressed tightly against the wall to see the bride tottering through the door, from the lane, helped this time by two women of the groom's family. She went up to her mother-in-law and another woman of her new family and bound folded headscarves round their foreheads. The bridegroom came out of the house and took the bride by the arm and led her to the bridal chamber, scattering coins with his right hand as he did so. Men and boys threw more coins from the roof and suddenly the yard was full of children scrambling like a wolf-pack for the coins. I was glad to be against the wall. After a moment or two the groom came out, to while away the afternoon by himself or with his young men friends. The bride sat in her room to be visited by her friends.

Down in the wide part of the street the *defci* was conducting the *çikacak*, an affair like an auction except that nothing was sold. She held up everything the couple had been given, coffee pots, teasets, money, and made jokes about them. She was a witty woman and everyone was laughing when they were not too busy totting up what everything was worth to the last farthing.

Next morning, the bride and another girl who had recently married into the family put on antique costumes and danced together in striped silk tight-waisted coats, fezes, coin coronets, and silk trousers. All of them were brought out of family chests and made a fine show. Then there was a feast, and the bridal was done; the little girl would have to start work, have to start being everyone's slavey.

Engagement parties are attended by all the grown-ups of both families. There may be dancing, there is certainly music, and two gold rings tied together with red ribbon are put on the fingers of the girl and boy. Then a speech is made and the ribbon is ceremonially cut. Each ring has the name of the other fiancé engraved inside it. I went to one or two engagements, but they are only attended by family and close friends while a wedding is open to anyone.

6

RAMAZAN

Ramazan, usually spelt Ramadan in the West, but always Ramazan in Turkey, is the thirty-day annual fast of Muslims. Its date is reckoned by the lunar calendar, the first year I was in Nar fasting began on 12 November and ended on 11 December, the next year it coincided exactly with November, and so on, moving about eleven days back each year. My neighbours told me God loved people who fasted, and that it was good for the digestive organs to rest them. All the villagers fast without question, in obedience to the will of God. I kept the fast with them.

One night the little *kandil* lights, like vertical rows of fairy lights, were on round the top of the minaret; Ramazan would begin that night. The fast, I read in a little booklet, was kept during the hours when a white thread could be distinguished from a black one. The fast was total, nothing to eat, nothing to drink, no medicine, not even an aspirin. Men must not so much as look at women with desire during daylight hours, let alone have any sex relationship with them.

A practical reason for the fast is that the going without food makes one know what it is like to be one of the very many undernourished in the world. The stomach emptiness isn't painful, especially for those who are used to it, but one's brain becomes mere cotton-wool, and one is incapable of reasoned action, of initiative. Besides that unpleasant effect, for me it had a good one, like a psychological shock treatment: during the long afternoons I only wanted one thing, food, and I knew that when the sunset cannon sounded I should certainly get it. After thirty days of that I emerged from the fast with a newly-washed and well-integrated personality. Turks are not neurotic and the suicide rate is very low, so perhaps the fast has that effect on them too, though they don't come to it as a discovery as I did.

Menstruating women are thought too impure to be allowed to honour God by fasting, though they must make up the days they have missed later when everyone else is eating. Midday meals are not served in residential institutions such as colleges or prisons, but the students and prisoners always have the pre-dawn meal, the *sahur*, served to them at dead of night. The evening fast-breaking meal is almost sacramental, a holy meal, and is called the *iftar*.

My friend Ikbal Hanım had a stomach ulcer and because she was worrying about whether she would be able to keep the fast it grew worse as Ramazan approached. I looked in on the first day to see how she was and found her lying on her bed in great pain, the unused digestive juices are very bad for stomach ulcers. I gave her a good talking-to and got her a diet-sheet, and she agreed to obey doctor's orders and not to fast; she went to stay with her daughter-in-law in Ankara to hide the shame of not fasting from her neighbours. She recovered and, keeping to a strict diet, no fat, no beans, even no tea during the rest of the year, now fasts with radiant happiness right through every Ramazan.

The many national daily papers bring out special sections for Ramazan, often written by eminent priests and scholars, but they have jokes too. I saw an old joke reprinted in one; it must have been from the days of the Ottoman Empire, for the drawing showed a policeman with raised baton threatening a poor fisherman with a net over his arm. The fisherman was trying to hide a cigarette but its smoke was rising from the cupped hand behind his back.

Caption:
　　Policeman: Why are you smoking in this Blessed Month?
　　Fisherman: Dear Sir, I am a fisherman, I must set my nets, and how
　　　　can I tell whether the wind is blowing from the north or from
　　　　the south and whether I can go to sea to fish if I don't watch the
　　　　smoke of my cigarette?'

Münevver told me that the canteen at Hacettepe, the medical university in Ankara, is almost as full in Ramazan as at other times, the students consider that fasting impairs their efficiency and they have a duty to their patients.

I was deeply asleep that first night of Ramazan, when I imagined my heart was beating very loudly, perhaps I was ill. Oh no, it's the drum they told me about, I thought sleepily. The drummer got nearer and nearer, stopped under my window; 'Get up, brother,' he bawled 'GET UP, BROTHER.' He must have had a special friend who lived opposite. I sat up and put my light on. Then the brother did get up and the drummer passed on down the hill. The drum was a very big one with a loud, low note, the skin loose in the cool night air.

Everyone got up, I peeped round my curtain and saw house lights everywhere. It was two o'clock. A woman in each house got up and lit the fire in the iron stove to warm the remains of the evening meal; she made some tea and perhaps fried some dough to eat with cheese. When the food was ready she spread the cloth on the floor over a table-board, put the food on it, and placed cushions round it. Then the household would rise and eat, then pray and go back to bed again to sleep. In winter the family all sleep in the same room to enjoy the warmth of the fire, they do not undress to go to bed, though women sometimes put on a nightdress over their day clothes.

I had no appetite at all the first night or two, but I soon got accustomed to it and made a good meal, with plenty of fats and proteins to keep me going. But my practice was not the village one, I loved the early morning hours and found them perfect for doing some writing. I would hear the Nevşehir cannon bang out in the last of the dark, then close at hand the sound of the loudspeaker in the mosque being switched on. The muezzin's call about the greatness and indivisibility of God would ring out loud and clear. '*Allahu Ekber . . . Allahu Ekber . . . Allahu Ekber . . . Laillaheillallah . . .*' It can be unbelievably beautiful. And then the foodless light of day would come and grow and fade again; towards five o'clock in the afternoon shadows would again possess the hillsides, and the remote peak of Erciyas Dağ would turn from pink to icy blue, to grey, and again the cannon would bang out to bid us eat our *iftar* together.

Fadime, who lived across the road and who had taken me to pray for rain, asked me to eat *iftar* with her family. Her handsome footballer son Memduh was at the door as I went in, posted there to listen for

73

the cannon. Fadime showed me along the corridor to her room where people were sitting round a low table-board which had a bowl of hot soup waiting in the middle and folded *yufka* bread and a spoon in each place.

Memduh came in when he heard the cannon. 'The gun's gone off,' he said, hurrying to his place and we began to eat. The radio was playing sonorous religious music, and we ate thankfully, starting slowly with a mouthful of helva or an olive or two. A good meaty stew followed, but Fadime had excelled herself in the last dish, pears stuffed with mince and cooked in grape syrup; truly Arabian Nights food, fit for Harun-el-Reschid himself, as I told Fadime. When we had all done, Fadime's husband stood up to begin his *namaz*; thin, with hollow cheeks and projecting jaw, he stood upright, his body in a pathetic zigzag, the pelvis tilted forward, the ribcage back, head and neck forward, his hands crossed before him: a man bowed by thought in the face of eternity.

The meal was simpler in the house from which Memnune's father had gone to Germany and left them with occasional money remittances instead of a man and father. A bowl of rice soup and a bowl of chicken soup were put on the table. The hot fat floating on the soup did something wrong as soon as it reached my stomach, and I began to retch convulsively, I had to scramble over a divan to reach the yard because I was afraid I was going to vomit. But I soon recovered and they said it was usual, if you thought your stomach was going to do that you should always start with something sweet, Turkish delight or helva. I didn't have any more soup but I enjoyed the *tandır fasulya*, beans cooked in a pot in the *tandır* ashes, with a good, tasty dried mutton bone and some tomato paste, a great Nar dish.

The Ramazan fast, or perhaps the winter weather, doesn't suit my landlord Haci Baba one little bit, he sits in the corner all the time with his face to the stove, sometimes with his eyes shut. Really, I think he is just pretending to be sleepy, and enjoys the noise of his lovely grandchildren round him without having to speak or take any notice of them. He always gets better immediately vine-pruning time comes along in March.

After the evening meal in my own house I sometimes went to sit with the teacher's wife with whom I had picnicked, the mother of the two Chinese-looking girls, Sabiha and Nurcan. The two girls were absolutely silent indoors, they brought us tea first, and when we had finished took away the tea-glasses and brought us at once small cups of coffee set on a tray. Nurcan's fringe of black Mongol hair fell over her eyes like a veil and made her seem even more shy and remote. One night there were other visitors, an older woman and three mothers of young families; four prayer rugs were collected and they decided to pray together. In Nar it isn't the custom for women to make a habit of praying in the mosque on every evening in Ramazan, though Ikbal Hanım and other Nevşehir women do. God, however, is more ready to accept the prayer and worship of a group of women than of one praying alone, so in Ramazan they like to gather in each other's houses. That evening the older woman was telling them how she planned to pray, and demonstrated some point as she sat cross-legged, bending gracefully and thoughtlessly forward to touch her forehead to the floor. She wasn't an athlete, just an ordinary woman of about seventy, her fingers thin and claw-like between their thick joints. They stood on their mats to start, hands folded over their breasts, heads bent, the older woman in front and the other three in a row behind. Then they all started to murmur the holy words and did thirty-three *rakets* straight off; it took perhaps half an hour or forty minutes, the length of one *raket* depends on the length of the passages from the Koran which are recited. The women have to learn them in Arabic of course, of which they do not understand the meaning, but every word is the word of God and that is all that matters. The three women in a row turned their heads and bowed to each other for the salute to the neighbours at the end of each *raket* . . . *Esselamun aleikum ve rahmet ullah* . . .'

When they had done they told me again that God loves those who keep the fast. Nurcan and her younger sister Lâle (Sabiha was away at Training College) brought in a great tray of apples beaded with wet, dishes of chewy grape jelly, shelled walnuts, pink and white boiled sweets and cool winter grapes. A copper beaker of water was passed round and we all drank to make up for our thirsty day.

Two of Memnune's sisters came to my house and showed me how

to fry dough made with powdered yeast; they made good doughnuts, light and crisp, a favourite dish for the night meal.

Towards the end of Ramazan I went to Mühüttin, the Headman of Nar, for the *iftar*, summoned by his young son who worked in the sawmill. It was about four when I got there and I sat with the men round the table-board for half an hour, waiting for the cannon to go. Men have the worst of it in Ramazan; in Nar they sit at the bare tables of the coffee houses; in Nevşehir, in the midday break from the offices, they stand about sadly in the street in their long black overcoats. Women can busy themselves with thoughts of the evening meal and preparation for it. But they must never taste what they are cooking, so that at any *iftar* you will hear the apology, 'Please forgive me if there is too much salt, or if perhaps I forgot to put any in.' I never heard of anyone cheating in Ramazan, they fasted for God. I didn't cheat either, once I couldn't think what to write exactly and took a cup of coffee but that washed out my whole day's fast. I told my friends that I had missed a day of Ramazan.

At the Headman's house the food was ready before the cannon sounded and the five small children were seated at another table and given food, the pregnant daughter-in-law sat with them to see that they behaved. Poor girl, she had to fast, though she had no room for extra food during the hours of darkness. Daughters-in-law are always given the jobs no one else wants, and they do them all with a willing smile to show how happy they are to be even the most junior and unimportant member of their husband's family.

When the cannon banged the men began eating. There were at least ten courses. When they had finished all the men but the young son of that Muzaffer who had gone with Fadime and myself to pray for rain went to the coffee house. I sat and looked at the dimly outlined figures of women washing the dishes in a room on a higher level; they were timeless and monumental and they might have been women in an etching by Rembrandt. When it was time for the men to pray in the mosque they dressed the lad up in a smart short overcoat and sent him out to pray with his elders.

We were free to play games; Muzaffer's party speciality was conjuring and the setting of puzzles. She tied a long girdle to a mug handle, gave both ends of the girdle to someone to hold and asked me to get the mug off the girdle. It was fairly easy, but I couldn't do the next; she tied both wrists of one girl together, and both wrists of another, with the tie girdles crossed. I found that same puzzle afterwards in a book for bright Mensa members; Muzaffer could not read or write. Then she did some conjuring, putting three raisins under the corner of a veil and that sort of thing. I don't understand it but I have seen it done at children's parties in England.

One of the best things about Ramazan is the courtesy of the men, when they met me they said '*Selamun aleikum*' ('Peace be upon you') and I replied '*Aleikum selam*' ('Peace upon you'). That courtesy extended to everyday life. I remember my last Ramazan evening well. I had been giving an English lesson to a hoca or priest, the assistant to the Müftü or head priest at the Big Mosque in Nevşehir, and we had finished at four and had an hour or so to wait before the meal. While he wrote at a table I looked out of the window and watched the sunlight fading from the vineyards on the hillside. The simple book-lined room was that of a good man. Muslims still love and fear God, while thoughtful people in England perhaps put love of neighbours first.

The most important night of Ramazan and of the whole Muslim year, is the Night of Power, the Holy Night when God revealed the Koran to his mouthpiece Mohammed. The first year I was in Nar it was a Sunday night, and the Sugar Festival to end Ramazan began on the following Thursday. I used the word mouthpiece instead of the usual prophet, because that is what the word *Peygamber*, translated Prophet, means to Turks. All the great *Peygamber* figures, Adam, Noah, Moses, Elias, Jesus and several more, were men through whom God spoke different parts of his unchanging word, but when the word prophet is used in English it has rather the connotation of someone who foretells the future, and is not very respectful; Old Moore is an example. In Nar I told them that I followed the order of the Prophet Jesus who told us to love God and our neighbour, but did not dare to add that on those two commandments hang all the Law and the Prophets. Starting an argument isn't love but a bore, and to Muslims a prophet comes first.

Most of the girls and women in Nar would be going to pray in the Big Mosque on the Night of Power, Haci Nazmiye, Haci Baba's wife, told me. She laid down the law for us all, and she said I could go too if I covered my hair completely and wore trousers or very thick stockings. She didn't offer to take me. When it was dark I put on thick green stockings and wound a big yellow stole round my head and went up the village. In the Meydan I saw a woman going to the Mosque and followed her, past a fountain where a youth was washing himself, into a room where many women were at prayer. I took off my shoes, looked round and decided I wasn't in the mosque proper and went through a door in the corner to the real mosque, where women I knew were among those praying. They waved me to an unoccupied space on the floor. I knelt on it, then sat back and looked round me. A golden-brown curtain separated us from the men and from behind it a man's voice had begun a talk about how pleasing to God it was when people kept the fast. He finished in half an hour, we heard the call to prayer from the minaret over our heads and the praying began. I couldn't take part for I hadn't learnt the prayers or movements, so I knelt a bit and stood a bit and said all the prayers I could remember and then composed my mind to reverence for God.

The women around me were utterly absorbed in their words and movements in unison, *raket* after *raket*, on and on, swinging to the floor to bang their heads on it, the *Allahu Ekber* they intoned as they did so muffled and booming, an echoing roar from the hoca or prayer leader and all the men and women. When they stood for certain parts of each *raket* I stood too and then I could see over the golden-brown curtain. Right up at the far end was the *mihrab*, a green niche corresponding to a Christian altar apse. (They use that same word *mihrab* for the little apses in the painted churches of Göreme.) The whole of the space on the other side of the curtain was as packed with men as our side was with women, all facing the *mihrab*, some in white skullcaps, some in black, some bare-headed. Up in front, by the *mihrab*, I could see the red-and-white turban and the pale blue shoulders of the hoca. The crowded men hid the rich fine carpets which no doubt covered the floor; cheap plain carpets were enough for the women.

As the women around me knelt I knelt too, upright like a picture I had seen of a knight at his vigil. All the women were so sincere, so lost in prayer, I made up a prayer to God asking him to give me the power and love to see them truly.

After about forty minutes the praying was done and the exhausted women sat back on their heels and mopped their streaming faces; the enclosed air was getting very hot. Another sermon began and Haci Baba's second grand-daughter, Ayşe, came in and found a place next to me. All the good ladies round, not as attentive to the preacher as they had been to God, wanted her to fetch them glasses of water from the fountain outside, so she was kept busy. I sat for a while comfortably leaning against the partition where the women had settled me, saying it would be comfortable for me to sit there. But I was tired and found the sermon hard to follow and the women were talking together almost soundlessly. I got up quietly and found my shoes by the door and went home.

The family all came home too after one more round of prayer. Haci Nazmiye was critical of my dress and said I should have worn trousers; the girls were wearing men's striped pyjama trousers. I explained that I had tried to dress in a decent and respectful manner as I would to worship God in a church, but she was not placated, she loved to give orders. Gülazar told me that all prayers said on that Night of Power are accepted, heard, by God. Emine Kozan, who comes into my story later on, was an old blind poetess in Nar, and one of her songs has a verse which goes thus:

> Döner çarkı felekler
> Arda inen melekler
> Kabul eden dilekler
> O Mübarek gecesi.

Literally translated into simple English:

> Heaven's sphere swinging
> Angels down winging
> Prayers acceptance winning
> That holy night.

Çarkı felek here means the wheeling firmament of stars which bring our fortunes, but it can also mean the flower we know as passion flower.

7

FESTIVALS

As my first winter approached I bought half a ton, five hundred kilos, of coal; a friend gave me an old sheet-iron stove and I bought chimney-pipes for it and fixed it. '*Kurdum*,' I could then say in reply to the greeting 'Have you fixed your stove?' 'I have fixed it.' My chimney-pipes went up through a hole in the roof and had a little galvanized hat on top, but most people's went out through the wall, sideways. The pipes should stretch right across the room before going out of the wall, so that no heat is wasted up the chimney and no rain comes in. The stoves draw better, too, that way, though I don't know why.

As October went on I heard drums and pipes, mostly in the lunch hour and late afternoon. One day I passed the Middle School play-ground as the band was practising—a big drum, clarinets and four little drums they called *trampet*. They were getting ready for the Republic Festival on 29 October, one of the secular festivals instituted by Kemal Atatürk, the Father of modern Turkey. Others fall in April and May and are also celebrated by displays given by soldiers and schoolchildren. Little Primary School children brought me poems praising Atatürk and their beloved Fatherland and asked me to copy them out neatly on my typewriter, they were proud of them.

The great day came at last. A little rostrum in the middle of the Meydan, beside the bronze bust of Atatürk, had been draped with red Turkish flags and the Primary children queued up to stand on it and read their poems into a microphone which had to be adjusted for height, especially for the first-year children who read first (Plate 5). All the Middle School children went around the Meydan in procession, following their band who wore special uniforms and were themselves led by their standard-bearer with a huge star-and-crescent flag, the pole supported by a leather holder round his waist. White-veiled mothers watched proudly, crowded on the Primary School steps and on the Mosque terrace.

The Commandos from the barracks across the valley had earlier gone into Nevşehir to put on a procession in front of the Province Governor on his dais. Afterwards they gave a display in the football stadium which we Nar people hurried in to watch; it was a battle piece in which mock forts were blown up and Turkish soldiers were martyred for the faith and had to lie under Star and Crescent flags pretending to be dead. The Commandos sometimes ran through Nar in formation, big sun-tanned young men, bare-headed and naked to the waist, singing in loud sweet voices, the front part and the rear taking the verses in turn.

There are two great religious festivals, the Sugar Festival (Şeker Bayram) on the three days immediately following Ramazan, and the Sacrifice Festival (Kurban Bayram) just over two months later. Both follow the lunar calendar. The Sugar Festival is the children's festival and they go round in groups dressed in their new clothes so that sweets can be given to them. As my windows opened on to the street I could throw them handfuls of sweets and nuts. All the houses were cleaned and the best carpets laid down; everyone had bathed three times from top to toe and put on new clothes. We visited each other or received visits continually for the three days.

The Sacrifice Festival is the time for the Pilgrimage to Mecca. Twenty-four men and women went from Nar the first year I was there; Haci Zelha, my neighbour, the mother of Mustafa the Middle School secretary, told me about the origin of the Sacrifice. Her daughters-in-law were listening too.

'God told the Prophet İbrahim that he wanted the most precious of his possessions as a sacrifice. The most precious? İbrahim thought and thought and searched his mind in agony. What could God want? His best ox? His new ram? His lovely camel? What?'

Broad, motherly Haci Zelha was a good story-teller. We felt anew for İbrahim. Tears gathered to our eyes.

'That night, the Prophet found the sure answer in the depths of his heart: his little son İsmail was certainly his dearest possession, so God wanted him. He must be sacrificed. He rose up, prepared the altar

F 81

laid the boy on it, lifted the sharpest of his knives to cut the child's smooth throat. He had laid the blade to the skin when a great light shone and the world about him disappeared from İbrahim's sight. He saw only an angel sent from God with a sheep, which was laid on the altar to be sacrificed in the boy's place.'

We, the listeners, sighed with relief. From that day to this, I understood, every Muslim family sacrifices at the Festival in memory of God's goodness to İbrahim, a sheep for one family, a cow for seven families.

Haci Baba, with six friends, was going to sacrifice a cow. The night before the Festival the *kandil* lights shone all night from the minaret. At sunrise I got up and dressed in clean clothes and saw that my house was neat and clean. Ayşe, the second girl of the family, came for me; I followed her to where their little brown heifer was tied up, shivering and defecating, in the yard; the children do not attribute human feelings to animals and were not sorry for her. A bucket-size hole had been dug in the ground to receive the blood, unclean to Muslims. The men from the seven families stood round the cow, and the children and I sheltered from the chilly wind in the house doorway; the sacrifice group was at the other end of the yard, by the big trough, which had an arched stone at the back of it carved with round sun symbols or flowers.

The men put a strap round the beast's neck to keep her horns out of the way, while they tied, first her front legs, then her back ones, together. They turned her over and dragged her into place so that the blood would run into the hole in the ground. Her big brown eyes rolled so far up that I could only see their creamy whites; as she continued to defecate Haci Nazmiye kept clearing it up so that the flesh would not be defiled. Haci Baba knelt at the back of the heifer's neck and stretched the throat out long. The other men knelt too and they all chanted three times:

'*Allahu Ekber ... Allahu Ekber ... La ... Illahe ... Illallahu ... Vallahu ... Ekber ...*'

One of the men rose and handed two knives to Haci Baba, who took one of them, and with it made the first incision into the throat he had been stroking. Blood began to run but the cow didn't struggle.

The next cut was deeper. She sighed. The slow cutting went on and on and the sighs had become groans before he had cut through the throat. Her blood streamed into the hole. When the windpipe was severed all the men knelt on her to press the air out. The killing must have lasted ten minutes and all the time the children watched seriously, in the way proper for a religious ceremony. When the convulsive kicking started I relaxed and took a deep breath, but not until the kicking stopped did the children say 'She has died.' Then Haci Nazmiye swept up a little coagulating blood and filled in the hole with earth.

I looked at the children and saw that someone had touched the centre of little Mehmet's forehead with a finger, leaving a spot of blood like a caste mark. I asked his mother, Nazmiye, what that was for, and she giggled a bit and said it would stop headaches. I thought. İbrahim had been prepared to give up his son to God, and God had been merciful. Nazmiye was gladly prepared to give up a part of her son to Gülazar, to share him with her, so that the boy might have two mothers and never be torn between them. And the spot of blood from the sacrificed cow showed that the boy Mehmet was under God's care as İsmail had been.

The cow's hide was soon peeled off and the still-twitching meat cut up and thrown into seven piles on some bamboo mats. Within the house the women prepared coffee for the seven men, pouring fresh water over the tiny cups so that they would be ritually pure, and boiling the coffee two cups at a time in the *cezve*.

Almost as soon as the coffee had been drunk the meat that they had put on to cook, the first piece chopped up small, was declared ready and we sat and ate it. Plain, no fancy cooking, not even tomato and onion, the usual ingredients of Turkish cooking. Afterwards the men said their thanks to God and went up to the cemetery at the top of the hill to pray at the graves of their ancestors. Most of the meat was given to the poor.

The following year Kazim would not let them fetch me for the sacrifice, for he thought it had distressed me. I was not aware that I had shown any emotion. The year after that, my last spring in Nar, they killed two sheep when the snow lay white over the yard. I wanted to record the important festival and photographed the red

83

blood and the white snow and the raven-haired children; like the fairy-tale simile for the colouring of the beloved, I thought. The children, well-schooled, watched the sacrifice quietly, though the sheep might have been a household pet (Plate 6). They were learning that everyone is in God's hands, and if he wishes we must all be prepared to give up what is most dear to us. He is merciful and compassionate. He may send an angel.

Part Two

THE PEOPLE

8

PEMBE

I was tidying the living-room when I heard a knock downstairs, a gentle firm knock, yet appealing. It was repeated. I ran down the stone steps and across the earthen floor, leaned against the heavy iron bolt to push it back and opened the big door slowly.

Standing in the sunshine, her face close to mine, was a thin, bent woman, neither old nor young. Hers was a good face (Plate 7); it was like a Gothic sculpture. Its many wrinkles had been chiselled by the blows of life on a virtuous character. She held out an offering for me, a bowl of soup held between her two hands. The soup was white, made from yoğurt, and green mint floated on its surface.

'Come in,' I said, but she would not cross the threshold.

Still smiling, she spoke, 'I brought you some soup for your breakfast, it's good.'

The delicious smell of fresh mint wafted up from the soup, I took a spoon from the table behind me and with the bowl in my hand tasted it once; it was indeed good. The woman moved politely back into the street and crossed a wooden footbridge to the door of her own yard.

Some days later I recognized her as one of two women sitting in the shade of the trees by the brook, her companion much older and shrunken to bird-like thinness. With downward waves of the hand they beckoned me to sit with them. I could understand little for I had not been long in Nar, but the woman who had brought me the soup was called Ayşe, and the bird-like old lady was her mother-in-law.

A girl spoke to me in the road between my house and Ayşe's; it was mid-day and heat and light were reflected from the road and the house-walls. Our feet were firm on the hot sand but our eyes were

87

half-closed, village and trees and houses lost in the blaze and shimmer of noon. She was Pembe (Plate 8), she said, grand-daughter, daughter's daughter to Ayşe who had brought me the soup.

'I am alone in the world,' she said. 'You are alone in the world. We must help each other.'

She wasn't tall, but slim-waisted, with shapely legs, about fourteen. She had rosy cheeks and dark intelligent eyes; her mouth was so pretty it was pleasant to watch her talking, though she was not self-conscious like most village girl-children, always looking with a silly smirk to see what effect they are making. Pembe was thoughtful and sensible, and, as far as I could judge, brave and mature. She told me her name, and its meaning; simply Pink, the colour. She was wearing a dress printed with pink flowers which she said her sister had sent her from Germany. She was learning English at Middle School, she had just finished the second year of the three-year course there. That was why we were able to help each other out in conversation, able to understand each other a little.

Only when she turned to go and said goodbye was her smile a little mannered, her eyes lighting up in schooled politeness.

She had a grandmother, then? A sister in Germany? Why had she said she was alone in the world? I myself had not been aware of being alone, I didn't feel lonely but creditably bold in breaking away from my life in England. She only meant I expect that we had not a strong man as head of the family to look after us. But was I lonely? I was stiff and shy, shut within myself, thinking of other people as I had been taught. Pembe, the little Muslim girl brought up in a different tradition, was thinking of me, thinking I was lonely. She had approached me and spoken to me, perhaps at her grandmother's prompting, but she had agreed with Ayşe and acted from her own good heart.

I had always wanted a daughter, perhaps Pembe could be, would be, almost a daughter to me.

I began to see her now and again, to walk with her to visit friends and to look at the Nar gardens, the rich plots of tomatoes and aubergines and peppers by the irrigation channels in the valley.

She was living with her adoptive grandparents, if that is the right way of putting it. The old couple, Ahmet Dede and his wife Pembe

(I shall call her Granny Pembe, it is a village custom to call girls after a grandmother, but it's confusing) had been married for some years but to their distress they were childless. They had no heir; their lands, and the big mulberry grove outside their tall house, would go to Ahmet's brother, the father of Haci Zelha's husband, Haci Zelha my worthy neighbour.

Ayşe, Granny Ayşe who had brought me the soup, offered Granny Pembe her daughter Memduha to adopt into her house and her family. Ahmet wanted a boy too, and soon they heard of a poor boy from one of the villages over by the Salt Lake; neighbours spoke well of him and he was adopted too. Ahmet and Granny Pembe then had two adopted children.

The surname of old Ahmet's family was Dede, meaning simply grandfather, but it was a new family name, one of those adopted under a law of Atatürk's which said everyone must take a good Turkish family name. The old name of the *lakap* or clan was the Hacilar. So Ahmet and his brother, the father of Haci Zelha's husband, and his sister Akgül, another close neighbour, were members of the Hacilar clan. It was I understood a very proud old clan.

When old Ahmet had married, he and his bride had lived in a tall old house built against the rockface, and they had hoped to fill it with their children. Granny Pembe had been a great beauty then. When they knew they would be childless they adopted Memduha and the village boy; girl and boy grew up together, fell in love and married. Brother and sister by adoption may marry under Turkish law, indeed the Prophet himself married his adopted son's widow; adoption is not complete as we know it. Adopted children always know their own parents and keep in touch with them if they can.

Because he was only adopted, Pembe's father had none of the pride and independence of the old Hacilar clan; he could never be an important member of the community of elders who discussed village affairs at the coffee houses on the Meydan. The indigenous Nar families, the *yerli* families, the important ones, could bully him, tell him what to do, but he was not one of them, could not expect their help at harvest or when labour was needed, nor the loan of a horse, nor the help of their wives when there was a cow to be cut up and cooked.

89

But I was told that Pembe's mother Memduha had been loved and respected by all, and I saw that her family still missed her much eight years after she had died from T.B. in the Ankara hospital. She had borne three children to the village boy: Neziha, Ekrem and Pembe the youngest. Neziha was about twenty-two and had made an unhappy marriage to a Nevşehir man; she had run away from him to work in Germany. Ekrem, the boy, had not been much good at school work and had not gone to Middle School; he was at present away working for some distant relatives in the south, harvesting grapes or cotton at Adana.

With the three children to look after, the lonely man had hastily married again; he had to have someone to perform the necessary household tasks. Turkish men are curiously helpless alone, they are never able to cook and keep house for themselves. As might be expected, the stepmother was the traditional stepmother; she wanted to push the children out and rule the roost. She had children of her own.

I began to understand why Pembe had said she was alone. However, Granny Ayşe was a woman of strong character and truly loving and thoughtful. Unfortunately Granny Ayşe had no male relative with her to give her a position in the village. Her husband, Mehmet Kaygısız, had been involved in a fight and had received a very heavy fifteen-year sentence. In the Turkish and old English idiom, he 'lay' in Nevşehir prison. His heavy sentence had been due to his quarrelsome nature, they said, and consequent unpopularity. Granny Ayşe had a son working in Germany and a younger one who was a policeman in Ankara.

Pembe proved her sincerity and thoughtfulness for me in a very practical way. When my lavatory began to smell I sprinkled Vim down it and poured in bleach, but it got worse and finally became blocked. I had thought that it would be emptied by the landlord for manure as in other villages, but no, Nar had a good drainage system. I had made a mistake and now things had got so bad I didn't know what to do. The neighbours complained about the smell but they didn't do anything to help and I didn't know how it was supposed to work.

I asked Pembe.

'That's nothing. What you want is a big tree.' That was what she said. 'I'll get one from Granny Ayşe's.'

She came back with a big long pole and stirred the hole around till it began to gurgle disgustingly. We were holding our breath. She kept stirring and it ran away slowly, the level dropped and I carried bucket after bucket of water to pour down.

'That's what you must do,' she said. 'Keep pouring water down, keep pouring water down every day, night and morning, and it will be all right.'

Haci Zelha's daughter-in-law came in to see that everything was all right, it was she who said the smell had got through to their lavatory. She saw the roll of toilet paper on a little shelf and opened her mouth in a gasp of understanding.

'Oh, that's what's the matter. You use paper, we use water. You really must keep pouring water down.'

I did keep pouring water down and since that day there has been no sweeter-smelling lavatory than mine in the whole village. The cleaning of it was dreadful, but since then I have known Pembe to be my true friend.

Pembe had told me several times that I must meet her friend Melahat, she was beautiful. She lived in an old house above the Meydan, next to the big Mosque. We had to go up a flight of broken stone steps and through a doorway in the wall, a doorway overhung by a vine. She came to the door at our first knock. Smiling, composed, in ordinary *dimi*, with warm brown eyes and pale creamy skin, she led us into a room with a fine rose-coloured carpet on the floor and modern well-used divans and chairs round the walls. She went into the kitchen and soon returned with glasses of tea for us. I glanced round and saw that the ceiling was of plain grey cement and the walls were patchy and discoloured and needed repainting. Our hostess was well-mannered, graceful and confident. I sensed something unusual, a mystery which needed explaining. There was a photograph on the wall of a clean-shaven elderly man with huge eyes, framed in chipped and tarnished gilt. A number of medals with coloured ribbons were tucked into the bottom edge of the frame.

We sat and talked and she told me her position. Her husband was a motor mechanic; they had come to live in this old family house in Nar to pay off the debts incurred in Ankara. The old man in the photograph, her husband's grandfather, had been through the First World War as a doctor in the army, when he had won the medals. After that he had been doctor to the Sultan's harem in Istanbul and had sought refuge here in Nar when the Sultanate had fallen. His antique lamps with coloured glass globes stood on the big sideboard; more old furniture was stored in a cellar cut into the rock below the house.

Melahat herself was a Laz, a member of a race which has inhabited the eastern end of the Black Sea coast from very ancient times; they were converted first to Christianity and then to Islam, but they have been Muslims for hundreds of years now and have forgotten the time they were not. They have fair creamy skins—in fact in colouring Melahat was a typical Laz—and when they leave their rich tobacco and tea plantations they become respected members of the professions in Ankara and Istanbul. But sometimes Turks make jokes about their funny accent, as the English may about the Scots; the Laz language is spoken around Rize on the eastern Black Sea coast but it is not taught in the schools. Melahat the Laz had no relations in Nar at all, so by Pembe's standards we were all three alone; her husband was not paying off his debts and he was not, I thought, good to her—she looked much older than her age of twenty-four. Her husband had family nearby, his uncle had been Mayor of Nar for years. He might be the black sheep but he was still a member of the family. Melahat did dressmaking in order to buy food for their two children, a little boy of seven who was staying with his grandmother in Ankara, and little Yeşim who came in to talk to us, a lovely child with long dancing legs and her great-grandfather's huge eyes. She was four; her name, Yeşim, means Jade.

The house was old; to prove it Melahat lifted a faded carpet in the hall to reveal a Byzantine cross cut into the central flagstone. It was roughly cut, each equal arm forked at the end; it might be fourth century, it might have been cut in any century when Nar was Christian. The Nar librarian and other knowledgeable men had told me that the old name of Nar was Nyssa. St. Basil the Great of Caesarea, now

Kayseri, had made his brother, St. Gregory, Bishop of Nyssa in the latter part of the fourth century. Why the place should now be called Nar is a puzzle; the word means pomegranate in Turkish and pomegranates don't grow there, they need a warmer winter. I thought about it sometimes: the most likely reason for the name seemed to be that a Turkish-speaking population had seen a painting of a pomegranate in the ruins of Christian Nyssa, and given the name to the place. The pomegranate was certainly used in Christian church mosaics of the fourth century as a symbol of eternal life.

Melahat and I stood looking at the cross cut on her floor; she asked me what it meant. I said it was the central symbol of Christianity because the Prophet Jesus whose teaching we Christians followed had been crucified on a cross.

'Oh poor Jesus,' she said in quick sympathy. 'Why did they kill him?'

'I think it must have been a put-up job between the Jews and the Romans who were in control of Palestine at that time.'

Pembe had left us when we were looking at the cross. Melahat took me to where a stream of clear sweet water ran into the yard from a cleft in the rock. We followed the cleft into darkness deep in the hill, waddling along with a foot on either side of the water. We had an electric torch. No light reached us down the winding passage, we could hear no sound of the rattling carts or the playing children. We came to a bath-sized pool cut into the rock; the torchlight made ripple patterns on the rock when we touched the surface of the water, so clear that it was invisible. It was not known who made the pool, nor why.

Pembe and Melahat and I were good friends. One day we put on our best dresses to go to a wedding, to a bride's house. Melahat had made her dresses and wanted to see how they looked. She herself looked pretty in a straight frock of string-coloured crochet; she had lived long enough in Istanbul to acquire confidence in her innate feeling for dress. In the wedding house we sat for a long time in a rock-cut room which became unbearably stuffy with the heat and the crowd of women. A mother came in to feed a baby in a cradle on the floor; she pulled up her blouse and bent over it and gave it the breast as it lay. The colours of the painted cradle swam before my eyes; I smiled at Melahat. 'Let's go.'

The air in the street was fresh after that hot room. We came to a tiny mosque whose minaret was reached by a diagonal flight of steps running up the wall. Pembe and I went in and admired the green-bound Koran on a shelf. Immediately inside the door I noticed a shallow uncarpeted depression.

'That's to wash the dead in,' said Pembe, following the direction of my eyes. 'See, there's the drain, here are the water jars and there is the board to put the body on and the box in which to carry it to the cemetery.'

'Who washes the dead?'

'Their family and friends of course. Who washes them in England? Don't you wash them?'

'No, it's all hidden, carpenters and nurses make a business out of it, it is not spoken about.' I felt ashamed; perhaps we in England turn our eyes away from too many real things.

There was a grove of mulberry trees just down the street from my house, the relic of an attempt ages ago to start a silk factory; it had been too cold and the silkworms had died. The trees remained, almost as tall as elms and bearing profuse sweet, white fruit, the first of the local fruits to ripen in early summer and very welcome in the village.

When it was ripe Pembe brought me a bowlful.

'Some mulberries from our trees,' she said with pride as she proffered them. The grove belonged to Old Ahmet, to Pembe's branch of the Hacilar clan. It lay between old Ahmet's house and Haci Zelha's.

9

THREE CLANS

The old clans, in Turkish *lakap*, are important in Nar life. If some shabby unshaven old man in patched pantaloons or some self-possessed pot-bellied old bundle of womanhood on a donkey is a member of an old Nar *lakap*, he or she is automatically given deep respect. It is a democratic aristocracy; all the old landowning peasant families have their own clans, often intermarried. That smooth, business-man type in a neat suit who would not be out of place doing some dealings in London is of very superficial account in Nar; he may be an official of some bank or Government board but important decisions about family or village policy are not discussed in his presence. The will of God about what is to be done is only made clear to the *lakap* elders after much humble discussion and meditation. They go to pray in the mosque, they go back to the coffee house. After a while all is made clear. The Headman Mühüttin was chosen by the elders and respected by the Government, while his opposite number, the Reis, or Mayor, Hakkı Bey, was thought a good man, but a Government official, not belonging, though he owned the mill. It was his job to provide us with our modern conveniences, like electricity and water and drainage and the loudspeaker and the baths. The Headman was the elder brother of Nar, in the beneficent Turkish sense, on our side.

Nar village is well governed; we all did our own thing if it was felt to be in accordance with God's will—I went ahead with establishing good understanding between Nar and England. We were not angels; the place by a stream where trucks were washed had a big notice saying: THE WASHING OF VEHICLES FORBIDDEN HERE.

Problems do arise, tensions, feuds between clans.

The house next to mine down the street belonged to the son of old Ahmet Dede's brother and his wife, Haci Zelha. Their two sons with

THREE CLANS

KOZANKIZI came from Adana province with her father more than a century ago. Her clan is still remarkable for the goodness and strength of character of its members.

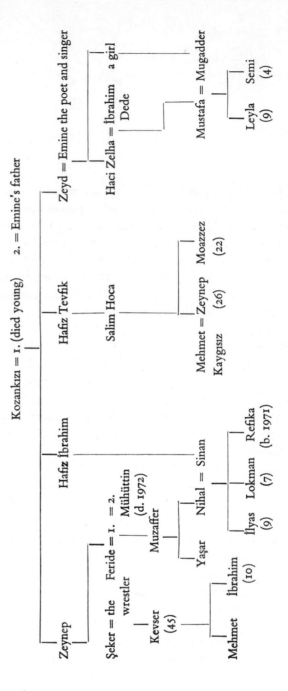

The HACILAR was an ancient and respected clan; they took DEDE for a family name.

The KAYGISIZ clan was ancient too, but they had a reputation for high spirits.

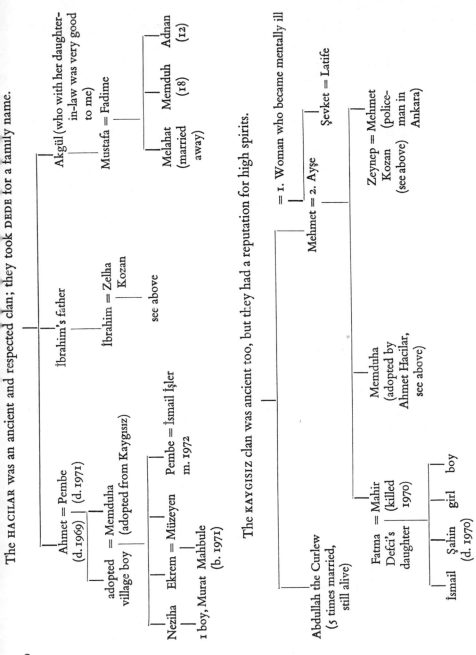

their wives and families lived there too. Haci Zelha, and of course her mother, Emine Kozan, who often stayed with her, belonged to the Kozankızı clan, or Kozan family. You can see from the family tree the many descendants of the Kozan girl (that's what Kozankızı means) whom I got to know well; many come into my story. A virtuous and strong character is a dominant hereditary characteristic among them all.

Haci Zelha told me how her ancestress Kozankızı had travelled to Istanbul and back on a donkey, fourteen hundred kilometres in all, staying in villages on the way. When her boy İbrahim had been learning the trade of watchmaker in a town fifty miles to the west she had loaded her donkey with goodies and travelled the lonely up-land road to see him. Possible bandits she met on the way were told that her two sons were just behind. They were, two little nippers. That boy, Hafız İbrahim, had been a watchmaker and a renowned preacher in Nevşehir. His son, Sinan, mended both my watch and my typewriter with swift and skilled fingers; he was married to Nihal, the daughter of my friend and neighbour Muzaffer, the one who had gone to pray for rain with us. Her mother, Feride, was married to the Headman.

Feride had had a sister called Şeker, whose daughter Kevser's house was on the other side of Haci Baba's house garden, where he kept his bees and where the black mulberry grew. One day Muzaffer brought her first cousin Kevser to see me and I liked her at once; she had only been to Primary school but used her reading skill to the full—I gave her books by modern Turkish writers which she read with enjoyment. She was the only grown woman I met in Nar who enjoyed reading. Her son was engaged to his cousin Lâle, and Kevser and I went out to help her husband's brother and his wife, Lâle's parents, to harvest their barley in a distant field. It was early summer; blue larkspur and pink daisies and yellow St. John's wort sprouted in bouquets from the pink soil under the apricot trees. Lâle picked us apricots to make jam, and when all the barley was cut and stowed in the cart we sat in the shade and ate watermelons.

Kevser and I walked among the flowers and tasted the apricots which had fallen from the trees, or which we could easily reach, and

we talked. Had I heard of her mother, who was called Şeker? I said
I had; the name Şeker is a diminutive and just means Sweet. The name
Kevser is the loveliest of all Turkish names, it is one of the rivers of
Paradise.

'She was tall and fine,' said Kevser. 'Her black hair hung as far as
her knees, shining and thick. Her voice was such that all thought it
should rightly be used in the service of God. So she recited the call
to prayer from the minaret. Of course women are not strictly speaking
allowed to do that, so she only recited the ones in darkness, the two
evening ones, the after sunset and the bedtime one. There were no
microphones in those days but everyone could hear her.'

'I wish I could have,' I said with longing.

'But she had enemies, one particular family of enemies, the quarrelsome Kaygısız family. They lived next door to her down by the fountain in our quarter, you know it don't you? She was *kus* with them,
not speaking, the families cut apart from each other by mistrust.
Şeker always had to carry a pistol in her belt so that she could have
defended herself against the Kaygısız if it had been necessary.'

'What happened to her?'

'She died when I was only a little girl, she had a big internal growth,
perhaps cancer. They cut it away, she came home and was very
well indeed for a while, then it came again and she died. She must
have been about thirty-five.'

Kevser is about forty-five and very handsome. I wondered if her
mother had been like her.

Şeker had married a big handsome wrestler from the village down
the valley. He was called up for his military service and she was left
with two little girls to look after. Harvest time came round and some
soldiers, the wrestler among them, went absent without leave in order
to help with the work. Don't forget that in Turkey the harvest is the
careful gathering in of God's holy gift; military service is willingly
given to the fatherland of course, but they made their choice of priori-
ties. A detachment was sent to look for the absentees, found them,
took them to Konya where they were shot without trial.

Haci Zelha was proud of her ancestress Kozankızı, of course, but
even more proud of the songs her mother Emine Kozan sang. Emine

had been blind for twenty-five years when I met her, but that had only made her sing the more. Then her husband Zeyd took up with other women and her heart became chilled, Emine said, so that it sang no more. But Haci Zelha and Muzaffer's son, Yaşar, Emine's sister's great grandson, had written down a number of her songs, poems, what you will. I suppose they might be called religious, anyhow they concern life and death. I wonder if I write a verse or two with a translation you will be able to see in them the sincerity, the true poetry, that I do?

> Ömrünün merdiveninden
> İniyorum yavaş, yavaş,
> Dunyanın her cıvarından
> Dönüyörüm yavaş, yavaş.
>
> Emine, ağlama derde,
> Azraile yoktur perde,
> Kimseye bırakmaz darda?
> Hep götürür yavaş, yavaş.

And the English, my somewhat lame version:

> From the steps of life's joy
> I descend slowly, slowly,
> From all the world's shores
> I turn, slowly, slowly.
>
> Emine, don't weep in grief,
> Azrael's face is open,
> Who can escape the narrows?
> We're all taken, slowly, slowly.

Emine sang that song first when she was over eighty; Azrael is the Angel of Death.

Haci Zelha was proud of her Kozan family ties and, warm-hearted, as she was, carried on Şeker's feud with the Kaygısız with burning loyalty, scorning them and looking down on them. Her beloved younger son, Mustafa, the Middle School secretary, followed her strong feelings with blind devotion.

Pembe, by blood Kaygısız, was a hardworking pupil at the Middle School hoping to do well and go into teaching. Her father was bringing his relations from the distant village into Nar, people without the same strict standards of right and wrong as those in Nar had. Pembe was the adopted grandchild of Haci Zelha's husband's uncle, and presumably she was part heiress to her grandfather Ahmet's possessions. There was pressure building up, a situation which must surely end in an explosion. What would happen?

10

A DEATH

Pembe reached up to a high shelf and took down a shiny little tray with a white cloth folded on it. On the cloth were two glasses of water and some cotton wool. Pembe's dying grandfather was lying under a quilt; she bent over him and offered him water, but he didn't want any. Then she moistened some cotton wool and tried to wipe the caked yellow mucus from his gaping lips. She wiped very gently and carefully.

The old man was fighting for breath, breathing in the rough rasping way that really can't go on for long. What was giving way, I wondered, the heart, or the lung muscles, or the blood-purifying mechanism? They said he couldn't eat or drink or urinate or defecate. He absolutely refused to have a doctor because he thought they had been wrong to cut off his leg years ago. All doctors were venal fools. He could refuse a doctor if he wanted to, he was a free man even if he was dying.

That morning Granny Ayşe had brought me some milk and had silently come inside the door and then bent close and whispered that Pembe's grandad was going to die. She seemed sure. Pembe had come to my house and fidgeted round restlessly, giving me her red hair-ribbon and then cleaning up, sweeping the whole house for something to do to take her mind off her dying grandfather.

In the evening, as she hadn't come back to take me, I had gone round and timidly entered the low, rock-cut room filled with the sound of unhuman breathing. It was on the side of the courtyard opposite the main house, whose three storeys clambered majestically, if shallowly, up the rock, reaching almost to the Headman's little square house, with the top turret of black basalt, that they said might be Byzantine. A stone stair scrambled up the side to the two upper floors, a stair with a vine hanging over it. In the dusk the courtyard was like a pit, with the evening sky at the top and a man dying a natural death in a cave at the bottom.

Pembe was trying to realize the fact of death; the man who had adopted her father and mother against the wishes of the rest of his family was dying, was going to leave them. Her gran, a vague dreamy old lady, racked with rheumatism, her father uncertain and timid with some sort of inferiority complex, her brother just young and ignorant, and her sister in Germany. And I myself, her friend and guest.

The family ducks came home from the stream and we saw that they were all right and put them into the stable for the night with the white horse and the young brown bull. She picked up the drake to show me and I held him and felt the thick down over his breast and his rounded thighs; the birds were like mallards but bigger and with splashes of white on their faded summer plumage.

We passed the hearth in the corner where the stepmother was bending over a pot of *bulgur* and went again into the room; there were carpets hanging on the walls in dull browns and purples and greys and oranges; Gran had made them a long time ago, using natural dyes. The only other decoration in the room was a red-legged partridge in a small cage by the door; he clucked softly and fidgeted on his perch. Good company, Pembe said.

A cloth was spread on the floor and we sat round it and ate the tomato-flavoured wheat; ordinary life went on but the coming of a death gave solemn awareness to everything we did, our actions were slow and almost ceremonial. The old man bent his head forward to try to ease his breathing but it didn't help. Pembe was quiet, as befitted a young girl, looking up sometimes at me, a guest from another culture, almost another world, whom yet she trusted.

Next day I stood talking to Gülten in the doorway between our houses, she in her long *dimi* outlined against the brilliant sunshine on the roof, her round dark eyes serious as they always were. The tall poplars rustled in the wind, a donkey slowly reached the climax of his bray, a cart rattled over rocks; the usual village sounds.

Unexpectedly and far from any appointed prayer time the muezzin began to recite from the minaret. We stopped talking to listen but I couldn't understand the sonorously drawn-out words.

Gülten noticed my blank face and said that it was the *selah*, for the death of a man who lived in our quarter and who had made the pilgrimage, she didn't know who it was.

'It was Pembe's grandfather, I was there last night and he was certainly dying. Do you think I should go round there now? What is the right thing to do?'

'Oh no, don't go now, they'll be busy washing him, then some men will carry him to the cemetery, perhaps they'll go this way and we shall see them from the roof. You should go this evening, that's the proper time.'

I went. It was dusk even in the street, really dark in the courtyard, but I could just make out the scatter of shoes round the door of the cave room.

A place was made for me between Haci Zelha on the platform at the far end, and the widow who was cross-legged on what had been the death-bed, now neatly covered with one of the soft mauve and orange carpets. Several women were there in everyday clothes . . . Granny Ayşe, my neighbour Fadime who was married to the dead man's nephew . . . I didn't know the others.

Pembe moved about, looking down, showing one or two more women in. The women took off their white *çarşafs* and folded them or hung them up before they sat cross-legged against the wall. They sat silent, formally present at the ceremony, not even meeting anyone's eye.

Haci Zelha was there because she was the senior female relative and a superb Koran reciter. She led the mourning, sitting cross-legged like a Buddha, her broad face too Buddha-like, but not her compassionate extrovert eyes. She began to intone, almost to sing. A prayer . . . a passage from the Holy Koran . . . a poem of her mother's on Death; holding out her hands in the lovely open Muslim attitude of prayer, palms up and opening towards each other. Her voice was strong, with a sort of rough richness. I began to be afraid I should cry. I jerked my mind away from thoughts of my own people who had died and looked up; tears were streaming down the faces of all the women . . . I didn't turn though to look at the widow beside me. Beside Haci Zelha, leaning over her, watching her mouth so as not to miss a word, was Granny Ayşe's mother-in-law, married into the Kaygısız clan, the feud forgotten in the closeness of death. The little bird-like woman was herself to die that winter, I didn't see her again.

Haci Zelha was lamenting the death of her husband's uncle, as was right and proper.

She stopped quite suddenly and we reached for our handkerchiefs.

All were quiet for a moment or two.

Then the widow spoke in a very loud voice, not singing, just speaking, a strong announcement unlike the whispered answers of a Muslim woman.

'After death comes the assessment.'

Again she sat still and silent; no one else spoke.

We sat on.

Presently two women got up to go, approached the widow, wishing that God might console her. Then they swung their *çarşafs* around them, white flapping moth-wings under the low rock roof.

Granny Ayşe beckoned me to leave with her.

By the double doors of the yard Pembe showed me the white well-scrubbed wooden board with short legs, up-ended against the wall, like the one we had seen in the tiny mosque.

'We washed him this morning, the board is all clean now ready to go back to the mosque.'

Early next morning Pembe came to my house and said they were going to a vineyard to turn the drying grapes, would I like to go with them?

Her brother Ekrem had the horse and cart outside; I sat in the back with a woman and her two children who got off when we reached their garden along by the river. We went on, the tall riverside poplars shooting into the sky beside us like green spears, and at Soğukpınar, the Cold Spring, we all got off and went up the hill to their vineyard on foot to lighten the cart for the horse. At the vineyard the horse was taken out of the shafts and tied loosely to the cart; he settled down to eat all the vineleaves within his reach.

We turned the bunches of black grapes which had been laid out on flat ramps to dry. One side of each bunch was already dry and those grapes had the hot Christmas taste of raisins. They had to dry for another week on the other side.

'Grandad was cutting these grapes with us,' said Ekrem thoughtfully. That was the only time that day that either boy or girl mentioned the death.

When they had all been turned Ekrem climbed a newly erected electricity pylon, climbed it to the top.

'Come on up,' he shouted, 'You can see everything from here, the whole world, all the villages and the big river in the valley and the snow on Erciyas Dağ.'

Pembe tried to climb but she didn't get far, the angle-iron bars cut her feet through her soft shoes. I watched, thinking how natural it was that they should feel loosened from accepted things by the shock of the death of the head of the family, how natural for them to feel free out-of-doors, away from the funeral atmosphere and the hushed voices of the grown-ups.

Ekrem backed the horse between the shafts and did up the harness. I volunteered to drive home; I felt myself a child again driving a pony-cart on holidays till our way was blocked by two donkeys, each dragging a bundle of dry beansticks on either side, the sticks all over the road. We couldn't pass; I pulled up, resigned to staying behind the donkeys. But madcap Pembe wouldn't have that, she leaned over, seized the reins from my hands, whipped up the horse and crashed over the beansticks which trailed in the road, breaking some and alarming both asses. We passed them, I barely able to express my anger adequately in Turkish, but Pembe and the horse were free and happy. Pembe kept the reins back to the village where I was put down at my house and went up to my room.

In a very few moments I went down again in response to a knock on the door and found Pembe there with a wide shallow sieve full of tight-rolled *pide* loaves. *Pide* are soft, flat loaves leavened and raised with old dough; they can be cooked in the same way as a pizza, with cheese, tomato and meat spread on top. She gave me one, saying 'Eat it' when I looked at it with surprise. She went on to take the remainder to all the neighbours.

I went upstairs and began to eat it, there was something hard inside and I unwrapped a lump of helva, the sweetmeat made from sesame and sugar, very crisp and good. I ate it, wondering what it symbolized, for it was the custom to take round such *pide* and helva after a death.

The caged partridge soon died, he only survived Ahmet for a day or two.

One day as autumn drew on I saw Pembe dragging her plough up to Fadime's door. I asked why and she said they wanted to borrow it to plant wheat. But friends told me later that Akgül, who was some sort of great-aunt to Pembe, as you can see from the chart, and was of course Fadime's mother-in-law, was very fond indeed of Pembe and wanted her for her grandson, Memduh, the handsome footballer. But his mother Fadime put her foot down, said 'No.' Pembe was good, Memduh was good, but Pembe's poor village relations wouldn't give the young people a chance of a happy and virtuous life and she for one didn't want to be allied with them. So that whole plan was put aside, though Akgül kept a warm spot in her heart for Pembe and watched to encourage any chance that might arise for her.

11

WINTER EVENINGS

When Ahmet's death had left her alone, Pembe's Granny moved her things from the cave to a smaller room across the yard, on the ground floor of the big house. It was easier to keep warm because some sun came in through the south-facing window. Like the rest of us, they fixed up their sheet-iron stove for the winter, setting it on a sort of tray with legs. Pembe made me get one of those for my stove too, she said everyone had them; I suppose they kept the ashes and dust together so that they were easier to clean up. Their chimney went up and then across under the ceiling, supported by wires, and out beside the window.

Granny said her rheumatism was very bad (Plate 9), she was giving up all work, she was old, her life was finished. She sat glumly cross-legged on her bed by the window, rolling a cigarette for a visitor if one came, and enjoying one herself. Pembe's brother, Ekrem, who had climbed the electricity pylon, slept on a high rickety bunk piled with all the bedding no one else wanted.

Pembe laid down her own mattress and quilt on the floor of the recess leading out of the old room, the recess which also held cases belonging to the sister in Germany. The old room was dismal and dark; there were some mouseholes at the bottom of the wall which were disclosed when the carpets and cushions were taken away. She showed me her corner, and the only pretty thing was a printed cotton nightie lying on the bed; Melahat had made it for her, I had bought the stuff.

The little room was indeed easy to warm, very cosy as the evenings drew in and the snow began to fall in November. School had of course started in September and I had made sure that Pembe had black ski-pants and black socks to wear with her shiny black overall, very crisp and smart with its white collar. The Middle School boys and girls also wore peaked caps with brass badges. After school had begun I went to the Dede house, to Pembe's house, as often as I could to help her with her English. I would go there on perhaps three evenings of the week. She refused to come to my house because she wanted to sit with her lonely old Granny as much as she could.

The yard door would be left unbolted for me and I'd go through it calling 'Pembe . . . Hello, Pembe,' and she would open the house door for me and let out some light so that I could see to kick off my shoes and set them side by side on the threshold. I would go in and take the old lady's hand in mine, her soft old blue-veined hand, smooth and cold, and kiss her on both cheeks. The kiss on both cheeks is the usual greeting between women who are friends and as it were sisters before God. It is a signal mark of love and respect to kiss a woman's hand and touch it to your forehead; that salutation can only be given to an elder. Children kiss grown-ups' hands. I have seen a girl student kiss the hand of the hostel porter who was an old friend; that surprised me but the other girls around took it for granted. 'Very polite,' they said.

Pembe would show me to a seat on Ekrem's high bed. Perhaps we would talk a little, there might be visitors in the tiny room, village women with henna-ed hair and fezes under their headveils, in red-print *dimi*.

Then Pembe and I would get down to work.

She had a little desk to write on, like a drawing-board with tiny legs. It could be put on her lap as she sat on the bed, or in front of her on the floor as she sat cross-legged. She had questions to answer for social science, or a map to draw for geography, a map of Turkey showing all the chief towns and with certain areas coloured according to what she was illustrating. She might do some maths, she might have an essay to write. I looked through her exercise books, each covered by her with bright paper so that she would know her own, and I was delighted by her conscientious and sensible work; how she had plodded on alone in that poor little room! She had her ailing granny to attend to, jumping up all the time to obey her orders. No one in the family but Pembe herself thought anything at all of school work, they could not read and didn't really see why it should be necessary. Ekrem had been through primary school; he was a typical, very pleasant boy who loved machinery; reading for him was the ability to read the instructions on machines.

During the half-year holiday in February the man who taught English at Middle School set them a short essay to do as a holiday task: subject 'The Visit'. Several girls came to me for help, asking me what the English was for so-and-so; they had no dictionaries. I had to try to estimate their teacher's vocabulary and I did my best for them, I made them learn the new words. All of them wrote about a visit to an aunt in Ankara or Istanbul. All, that is, except Pembe. Her essay was an imaginative one about a walk along a winding path through a wood, then she came to a lake among the trees and in the lake was an island. She longed to go to the island but she could not find a boat, though ducks swam quacking on the water under the trees.

While Pembe was writing I looked round me at their room. A patchwork quilt hung on one wall, and beside it a calendar with red roses on it and a mirror with all the family photos stuck in along the bottom. They pointed out the photo of Pembe's mother with blank, staring dark eyes. It is considered the correct thing for Turkish women to put on that blank look for photographs, they are never smiling. The patchwork quilt had been made by her, by Pembe's mother, Memduha. It hung there to cover a hole in the wall which connected the room with the stable, where Lightning the horse lived with a young bull and the family of ducks. The stable door was out in the yard. The Government does not like such an arrangement; the villagers do, especially for the winter, the animals give out warmth. I myself was reminded of the Nativity, but I found the story was quite unfamiliar to the Nar people. I told Mugadder, Haci Zelha's daughter-in-law, that in my part of England there was an old belief that all the cows in the stable knelt at midnight on Christmas Eve, because on that night the Prophet Jesus had been born to Mary in a stable. She accepted the kneeling as perfectly natural but was quite shocked at the stable ... 'Oh, the Prophet Jesus wasn't born in a stable, he was born in a fine house, a palace perhaps.'

When our lesson was done Pembe would ask me if I would like

some coffee and she would boil it on the Primus which had a cobweb of wire across the top to support the *cezve*, the tiny coffee saucepan. She squatted by the stove pumping away; she made very good coffee, hot and sweet.

She did not see much of her father and stepmother who had their rooms on the floor above; they knocked on the floor if they wanted anything, Pembe to feed the horse, shut the stable up . . . anything like that. The sister in Germany sent Pembe and her Granny occasional parcels of dress materials and stockings.

Then her father fell ill with a stomach ulcer which haemorrhaged; he was sent to hospital in Kayseri for treatment, perhaps an operation. I went to Pembe's house for news and found Granny Ayşe kneeling with her head on the other Granny's knee, both weeping bitterly. The hurt at the death of Pembe's mother, whom they had loved dearly, had come back to them; they feared the loss of the man, the breadwinner. However, he recovered with treatment and came home, and when the weather improved he found work in the rope factory in Nevşehir, a big new works with a night shift, on which he held a supervisory job. He would come home in the morning and after breakfast go straight out and do what he could in the fields without sleep; many villagers compromised in that way but in the long run the gardens and vineyards became neglected. He was a good fellow really, he wanted to do his best. The stepmother was no good to him at all.

Pembe and her Granny missed her mother and asked me to get some earth from her grave in Ankara so that they could mix it with water and drink it. That was an old village remedy for heartache. I didn't get it but I resolved to do whatever I could for Pembe. She thought that her best way ahead was in her books; if she did well in her exams she could get a place at the Teachers' Training School. Melahat said I could help her family as part of my Ramazan duty and they would accept it simply and without loss of pride as though it came from God, so I gave her Granny some money and bought a dress-length for Pembe, warm flannelette printed in blue and yellow swirls, like feathers.

Granny talked to me sometimes. She remembered Christmas parties in Nevşehir with lots of lovely food, and weddings bright with candles. Her particular girl friend had been Christian but all the Christians had had to leave Nevşehir in the exchange of populations under Atatürk; Muslims had come in exchange from Janina and Salonica and Rhodes. I met some, they loved to talk about their old homes. In her middle years Granny had made heaps of carpets, spinning and dyeing her own wool. I often saw a couple of old women spinning together, in a sunny corner in spring or in a breeze on the hilltop in summer. They would ask me to judge their threads, which was the finest and most even. Their mothers had beaten them for spinning unevenly when they were little girls, they told me; it was a waste of wool to spin lumps. A fine thread would be for socks, a coarse one for carpets, but they must be even. A woman used to spin in the evenings at a house across the road, where I sometimes sat; she would stand near the wooden post which held up the middle of the ceiling and swing the spindle, throwing it far from her so as to twist the thread evenly. I liked going to that house, the housewife had a rough voice but a radiant personality.

Haci Nazmiye used to sit spinning in my landlord's house, the coil of teased wool waiting to be spun wound round her left arm. It was there I heard the best stories, *masallar*, long rambling children's fairy stories. Gülazar told wonderful ones, it was her special social gift but she wouldn't tell them if her husband or her father-in-law were in the room. She was shy and she wanted to throw herself into the telling, forgetting everything else. Of course they have never been written down.

A woman was left alone while her man went on a long journey; he was at last given up for lost and she worried about how to find a husband for her little girl. A bear came to the door and asked for the girl. She refused. He came again; again she refused. The bear said that the next time he came he would take the girl whether her mother agreed or not. They were frightened and barred the door securely, they didn't know whether the bear wanted the child for food or as a wife but either would be terrible. They had to go out to the spring for water and one day there were two soldiers in shining armour there. A fox came up and the soldiers told the woman that the fox

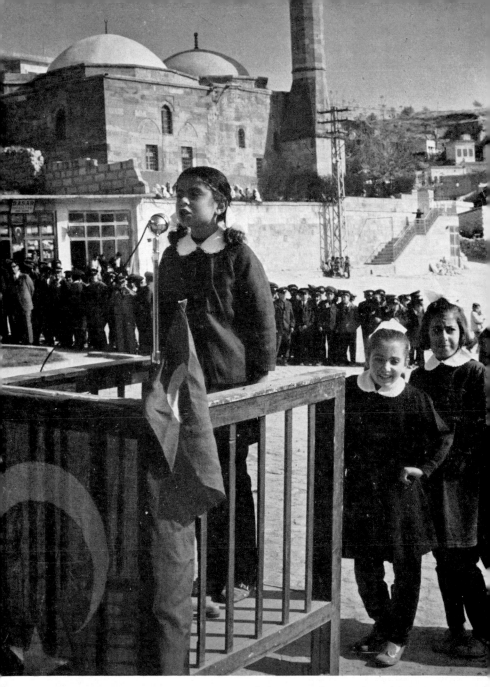

5. 'The Primary School children . . . read their poems' (Mustafa Dede's little daughter)

7. 'The woman who had brought me the soup was called Ayşe'

6. Haci Baba's granddaughter, Zelha, with a pet lamb

would help her. When the bear came the fox took dust from a camel's footprint and threw it at the bear, and the bear disappeared.

That was one incident in a long story. I can remember more of the story of the three bearded brothers. They lived together, three long-bearded bachelors. A traveller came to their door and they gave him hospitality for the night; he told them all about the wonderful places he had seen. Next day, when he had left, they paid their debts and ordered their affairs and set out in search of wonders . . . They came to a fine city with all its shops and warehouses stuffed with goods and not a man to be seen anywhere. For some time they lived on the fat of the land, helping themselves to what they wanted.

One day the youngest brother was poking idly with a stick in the dry earth and the sand fell away leaving a hole through which he saw a fine bathhouse, its dome decorated with rich pictures. There he saw three beautiful fairy women bathing themselves. How lovely they were . . . the youngest of them protected the youngest bearded brother from the misfortunes which befell his brothers. The youngest man on his way home fell in with a caravan of travellers but they lost their way; they saw a shepherd with his flock and approached him to ask the road. The youngest brother went up to him and the shepherd bowed his head towards him to see him, for his eyes were in the top of his head. His name was Tepegöz, meaning Summit-eye. Evening was approaching and Tepegöz was hungry so he picked up a man and ate him, sucking the bones dry and throwing them away. The travellers didn't know the way out of that place and the next evening Tepegöz ate another of them, again sucking his bones dry and throwing them away. The youngest brother thought something had better be done, so they made two skewers red-hot in their cooking-fire and stuck the hot irons into Tepegöz's eyes while he was sleeping. He yelled, mad with pain, and crawled about feeling for them, but the youngest brother escaped by dodging under the belly of one of the sheep.

He was utterly lost. He wandered into a cave for shelter and in the windings of the cave he was more lost than ever; it was pitch dark and he was about to commend his soul to God when a fox came up to him and told him to follow him. He did this and the fox led him up and up and up, till at last they came to the light of an opening in a hillside.

The youngest brother looked fearfully out and when his eyes were accustomed to the light he saw a bay of the sea rippling in the sun; round the bay were green hills, and by the water, among the flowers, lay the same three lovely fairy ladies who had befriended him before . . . Well, he had more adventures but of course he got home in the end and his friends came to welcome him. The hoca from the mosque asked him if anything wonderful had happened to him.

'Nothing,' he said. 'Only my beard grew a little longer.'

Gülazar has as much right to her version of the story as Homer had to his. It happens that his version has become part of our cultural background in Western Europe.

Gülazar told stories; Haci Baba on the other hand had a literary approach. He had an old book printed long ago in the Arabic script.

'Who was Belkis?' he asked me one evening, holding the book open.

'She was the Queen of Sheba,' I replied, 'and she came from far away to visit the Prophet Solomon.'

Haci Baba smiled with great pleasure because some part of our religious tradition was the same. 'But we say she was Queen of Sana,' he said politely. He went on leafing over the book. 'Did I know the story of how Solomon sent a cuckoo to her with a letter? For of course he knew the language of the birds. The cuckoo flew to her window and tapped on it with his beak and gave her the letter.'

'No, I never heard that.'

'He had her, you know,' said Haci Baba, with a rather cheeky sideways look.

'Yes.' But anxious to defend the honesty and virtue of the famous pair I added:

'Did you know that their descendants were the rulers of Abyssinia, indeed still are?'

Then he asked me, still leafing over that book, if I knew that the Prophet Jesus could talk as soon as he was born.

'No, we have no record of that, but we know he defeated all the wise men in argument when he was twelve.'

'Of course, he knew everything,' Haci Baba answered simply and firmly.

I had fun with the women and children remembering nursery

rhymes, once I had been put on the trail of some to start them off.
There was:

> *Haci Baba tintin*
> I found five farthings,
> I went to the shops,
> There was nothing there.
> I went to the market,
> There was nothing there.
> I boiled some milk,
> There wasn't a spoon.
> A guest came,
> There wasn't a mattress.
> The baby cried,
> There wasn't a cradle.
> I came to a house,
> There wasn't a housewife.
> I came to the mosque,
> There wasn't a preacher.
> I came to the stable,
> There wasn't a donkey.

They had a rhyme for the fingers, like our 'This little piggy' for
toes. It starts with the palm of the hand, then comes the thumb and
so to the little finger:

> Here came a bird,
> This one caught it,
> This one killed it,
> This one ate it,
> This one came home from school,
> 'What's for me? What's for me?' he said.
> 'Bones for you, bones for you,' said this one.

12

SPRING; THE LETTER

On the bare hillside the flowers of iris persica were little flames in the sunshine. *Navruz* it's called, the Persian word for the New Year which in Iran is reckoned from the Spring Equinox, 22nd March, when the flowers open. Its transparent fragile mauvish or yellowish petals were almost invisible till the sun shone through them; each flower had three dark purple, velvety falls and three orange beards like little crests. Ayşe and Zelha, Haci Baba's grandchildren, ran about collecting a bunch of them; they grew singly and were hard to see. There was Grandfather Haci Baba down below pruning the vines, and Gülten filling the donkey's bags with fresh green weeds for the stock and carefully gathering some small mustard plants to provide vitamin C for the family, too.

Spring had come, towards the end of March. As we all went along the path back to the village the little girls ran aside to collect the pleasant red or yellow fruit of the Asian medlar, a sort of hawthorn whose tiny apples are kept in cold storage on the ground by its own fallen leaves.

Fadime, Memduh's mother, admired my *navruz* with three deep purple petal tips on each flower and made me touch them to my eyes as I recited the Unity verse of the Koran:

'*Kul fi Allahu ehat, lemyellit ve lemyulet ve lemyeku kufuven ehat*' . . . 'Say, God is One, he was not begotten, nor has he begotten any. God is one.' A month before I had found some of the pale pinkish crocus, the very first flower of the year, and she had touched them to her eyes and made me do so, saying, 'May God be in my eyes, may my sight be blessed.'

Spring had stirred up the men all over the village; they were pruning, buying pigeon dung, selling onion sets and raisins. They keep the raisins by them through the winter because raisins will maintain life if there is no other food.

Pembe came to me one day much troubled; her Granny had had 'flu like most of us, but instead of getting up after six days or so in bed she had lain on, depressed and groaning with her rheumatism and wanting to die. Now on top of that they were infested with fleas and Pembe and Ekrem couldn't sleep either.

'Heavens, that won't do,' I said. 'I'll come round on Wednesday afternoon, your school half-holiday, and we'll start on the cleaning straight away and finish by evening, that is if God sends us a sunny day.' I remembered Pembe's help with my lavatory; perhaps I could repay it.

At mid-day on Wednesday it was brilliantly sunny; Pembe was ready for me and we pulled the old bunk bed to pieces and threw it into the yard, threw all the cushions and mattresses after it into the sunshine, then took Granny out and settled her down too; the sunshine would be better than anything for her rheumatism, we hoped. We sprayed everything with fly-spray until the yard reeked of it and washed the floor with a disinfectant solution. Then we took all the carpets down to the fountain below the road, used rags to plug the outlets of the biggest of the stone troughs, flung the carpets into it and trampled them; then pulled them out and beat them on the concrete with the beater I borrowed from Gülazar. We went on until no more dirt came out of them and they no longer smelt musty, but clean and sweet. Then we hung them around in the sun like red and yellow and purple flags; they hung from Granny Ayşe's footbridge, they were spread on her woodpile and on the parapet by the stairs in the old family house. One or two were dry by evening; we spread a sheet of polythene over the damp floor, just for a day or two, and covered it with fresh carpets, put the bunk bed back lower like a divan, put Granny's couch back by the window and looked round with satisfaction at the clean room. We'd done Pembe's alcove too. They had no more fleas and slept well after that.

Pembe was working steadily and hard at the Middle School, and she thought a lot of Nesrin, the Assistant Head, adoring her shyly from a distance. Mustafa Dede, Pembe's grandfather's great-nephew, was the Middle School secretary. The one-time Head, Harun's friend, had gone to do his military service and Nesrin had been in sole charge for two or three months until a relative of Mustafa accepted the post of Headmaster; he had been teaching in the southwest, and had married Mustafa's wife, Mugadder's sister. He and Mustafa worked hard at the school. It is very easy to imagine how they must have banded together against Nesrin, the woman Assistant Head, to them a mere woman, a lower being, inferior to males by her very nature. She had a hard job and looked more and more nervous. Fortunately, Naim Bey, the science master, saw her at her true worth, loved her, and her father, Latif Bey, agreed to their engagement. Latif had got a transfer from the directorship of a lovely little town near Kayseri to that of a dreary village near Nevşehir so that his wife could keep house for both Nesrin and himself, and she did just that, but she spent most of her time in Nesrin's pleasant flat on the Meydan in Nar. Two of Nesrin's brothers lived there with them, and one of them went to the Middle School; there was a little girl at the Primary School. They had other boys, all at university or technical college; Nesrin certainly had wonderful parents in that they had given her an equal chance with the boys.

As May Day approached people made plans for the public holiday on that day. Nesrin organized a Middle School outing to a big electricity project in two minibuses. Pembe told me about it enthusiastically and I asked her to get tickets for both of us. Then a strange thing happened, little Ekrem said he 'wouldn't send her', forbade her to go. By village custom she had to accept that totally unwarranted interference with what would have been an educational visit. Ekrem was very young and immature and at first I was really ragingly angry. How dare he? But Pembe and dear Granny Ayşe calmed me down, saying we'd all have a lovely picnic in the woods instead.

May Day is an old spring festival and it has nothing to do with Labour Day. It is not much like the May Day of the old Welsh poems either, a May Day when young men and girls went into the woods and forests to sport together. The picnics were family affairs, though perhaps boys and girls could look at each other in the company of their families and even wonder very tentatively if they might some day get married. It was traditional to eat beans on May Day, beans in the woods. Good Nar-grown beans, cooked with oil and tomato sauce and a tasty mutton bone. We were going into the woods, the poplar groves and under the great spreading walnut trees, their leaves at that early season still golden-green; we'd find a picnic place under the willows by the brook or where the apples were hiding their green fruit in an orchard by the cliff. We found people in all the places we had hoped for but at last we came to a grassy spot by some hazels and wild almonds. Pembe and two of her girl friends made a swing from chains used to tether donkeys and swung till they were tired. Then we sat on the grass and ate the dish of beans which Ayşe had heated on a fire; they were delicious.

Ekrem came and played ball with the girls, and a pleasant little grandson of Ayşe's played with us too, he was called Şahin, and was about eleven years old. We went up to the top of the rocks where we could look down on the waterfall, where the girls picked yellow roses and stuck them in their hair. Everyone around was happy, enjoying themselves, forgetting all their troubles in the mild sweet air among the wild roses and the furry-leaved buttercups and the clumps of pink sage.

On most afternoons of May we had rain; more and more flowers blazed in uncultivated corners round the valley and on the slopes. Scarlet and orange poppies, yellow woad, pink dog-roses, yellow senna. Pembe was happy about her school work for she had had very good marks at the February half-year and was confident about school—she sat working at her schoolbooks every evening and worked in the gardens at weekends and half-holidays. She had every reason to think she would have a good Diploma to show her sister when Neziha arrived in June.

One day I met Pembe on the road and she didn't speak, didn't look at me.

I supposed she was busy, thinking about a lesson, and I was busy too and did not go round to see her for a few days. But something had happened.

Mustafa adored his mother even more than Turkish sons commonly adore their mothers. She was first in his thoughts; if she were ill he nursed her, if her back ached he massaged it. She herself was glowingly fulfilled in her devotion to her family; she did the heavy field work in the burning sun herself, rather than send her sons' wives out to be prematurely shrivelled by it. She wanted them fresh and smooth for her boys. She and her husband insisted on the old Muslim rule that the girls must always be heavily covered; no man must see them. But she was much respected and indeed loved in our quarter; she would sing her mother's songs to the dying or those in grief.

Mustafa was a lordly male and the apple of his mother's eye.

And all that winter, when there was no Head and Nesrin was Deputy Head, the lordly male had had to take orders from a slip of a girl, or lose his job. Take orders, from one of the soulless playthings created by God for the solace of males. Bitter resentment grew in his mind till he almost burst. Then his brother-in-law comes to take up the post of Headmaster; they are the best of friends, his amour propre begins to sit up and feel better.

He comes out of his office one noon break, walks two steps to the corner of the corridor where he can see the main hall lit by the sun-shine streaming in through the door. Hm . . . there in front of the placarded notice board is a boy, Nesrin the Assistant Head's young brother . . . here comes Pembe Dede from the other classroom round the corner, and Mustafa draws back into the shadows. He sees the boy's lips moving.

'Oh Pembe, I've done all those maths problems ready for tomorrow, my elder brother has checked and there are no mistakes. If you like borrow my book now and give it me back tomorrow morning.' Mustafa is looking at his bright eyes and moving lips. Boys and girls swirl between them. Pembe looks down, hesitating for a moment, thinking what is the right thing for her to do, for Turkish school children accept each other's help. (The purpose of education there is to teach facts, not to develop mind and personality.) But to speak to a boy is wrong, though she knows her maths is weak; the correct answers to those problems might tip the balance of marks enough to give her a chance . . . but she is a good Turkish girl, God-fearing, she has had to avoid the silly lad, it was he who was the cause of her missing the May Day outing. She tilts her chin up in a firm negative, clicking her tongue to stress it, but keeping her eyes down. Turns on her heel, walks out through the door.

Mustafa, back at his desk, gives himself up to thoughts which flame through his mind. Just like a Godless Kaygısız to ogle Nesrin's brother . . . she probably indicated a rendezvous for tonight when I couldn't see her. Somebody should know about this, what will happen if things go on? Somebody should tell Pembe's father . . . Suppose he knew, what would he do . . . do to Nesrin's brother? Perhaps the whole of his family, Nesrin too, might have to leave Nar. Somebody should tell Pembe's father . . . who? Why, it would naturally be the job of the School Secretary. He must, it was his God-given duty. The cover comes off the typewriter, the apparently official letter is written saying that Pembe has made improper advances, done bad things with Nesrin's brother. They must have done, how could they do anything else, the female monster's brother and the Godless Kaygısız girl? Dreadful that he, Mustafa, should have to work in a school with such people.

Pembe came into her house, her father took the gun off the wall to shoot her. She stood stunned, trying to accustom herself to the enclosing walls of hate and mistrust which were foggy yet impenetrable. It was the end of her innocent tomboy childhood but, thank God, not the end of her life. They checked her father, stopped him; he was satisfied with her promise that she would never speak to the boy again. Poor little down-trodden man, unable to assert himself among the village elders, his honour apparently destroyed; he didn't see Mustafa's motives, he believed the letter.

Pembe's mind was completely busy with wondering what she had done wrong, she couldn't think of anything else, it was just before her finals, the exams which were to lead to her being a teacher, the exams she had worked so hard for all her time at school. She got through a week of misery and then failed in maths, English and social science.

I found out all this bit by bit, Pembe dared not speak to me; she thought perhaps her father objected to her seeing an infidel, and I could have done nothing. Certainly I knew Pembe was innocent of any interest in sex, and I didn't realize that the villagers were so down-to-earth that they were doubting Pembe's virginity—well, some were, just the men who didn't know her. They are perhaps a little lacking in imagination, they didn't realize the strength of Mustafa's hatred of taking orders from a woman. Pembe's roots and her life were in Nar, I was, alas, a stranger, in the dark about what I could do and how. In the event I just continued to trust Pembe, I was ready to help her in any way. She would have two more chances of taking the exam, in June and in September.

Pembe settled down to working every day in the fields, taking out the dung from the stable, drying it and spreading it on the gardens, and sticking beans and doing everything that had to be done. Her relationship with her grandmother was bad, the family regarded her as a naughty girl, dismissed the unpleasant subject from their minds, thought no more about her. They used her as a workhorse, without feeling. Never gave her a kind word . . . not that she wanted a kind word, she had my respect anyhow, and Granny Ayşe's. The rest of her people went ahead with plans for a wife for Ekrem, a wife from the village by the Salt Lake where his father came from. Neziha, his sister, would pay the heavy brideprice out of her wages for working in Germany for a year and a half. They plotted, waited for the return of Neziha.

Grandmother and Pembe spent every evening looking at the yard door expecting to see Neziha walk in, but their hearts grew sick when she was already a month later than she had said.

In Haci Baba's family life moved on like a quiet river of serene content; they enjoyed work, tending gardens, cleaning the house and preparing coffee for guests. They didn't look forward or back but were alive to every minute as it flowed past them.

We were standing under the black mulberry tree at the bottom of the garden watching the Middle School pupils come back from an end-of-year picnic in the woods. Little Mehmet was all dressed up in a long blue robe Gülten had made for him, and on his head was a round white cap with its band embroidered with sequins. It was the day of his circumcision. The only guests were some relatives of Haci Naz-miye's. That was unusual; perhaps they didn't want people because of the two wives. They were rather a quiet family socially, though much respected and well off by village standards. We had gone out into the garden to leave the guestroom free for the men to have a meal in, Osman Effendi, the Health Officer, among them. Mehmet was proud of being so important but sometimes he'd stop smiling and look apprehensive. We looked among the green leaves for the first of the mulberries to be really black and ripe; they had a very strong rich taste a bit like sweet loganberries, quite different from white mulberries. We admired the way the bees were working, and the crowds of them at the entrances of the cow-dunged wicker hives. There were flowers in the garden too; the girls picked two scarlet snapdragons and stuck them in Mehmet's cap-band like perky little feathers.

Then we were called in and sat down round a table-board in the guest-room and food was set before us. Gülazar and Nazmiye ate with us but Mehmet had been taken to the bedroom.

He screamed 'My Mother, oh my Mother' twice but Nazmiye and Gülazar didn't lift an eyelid, pretended they hadn't heard. I couldn't eat.

They called us. Gülazar went first and sat cross-legged on the bed beside him to comfort him and wonder at him, now a man. Haci Baba smoothed his pillow. Tears were rolling slowly down Mehmet's face but he had stopped crying though his face was flushed. The toy motor car I had given him was on his pillow within reach, he could lift his hand and touch it. His round cap was under the quilt to hold its weight up off his sore body. Soon his sister brought an old straw hat to replace it and the pretty cap was put beside his head on the pillow.

It was a great day for the whole family, the initiation of the precious grandson into manhood.

Next day little Mehmet was walking about almost as bright-eyed as ever. The soreness went and they made him a fine new trouser-suit; his father took him up to the coffee-house and sat down proudly with him at a table.

13

NEZİHA AND NESRİN

Neziha has arrived. In the old Dede house food is being prepared for the travellers. The girl they hope is to marry Ekrem has come from the village; she strides about the yard, long plaits banging on her buttocks as she hurries to prepare vegetables and get water for the cooks. Her mother and other women are in charge.

In Granny's tiny room a new German tape-recorder roars away; family voices, scraps of pop music. Smoke wreathes up from long fat German cigarettes. Granny looks lovely, almost as in her youth, in a brown cardigan. Neziha sits against the wall in a bright silver waistcoat of leather fabric, sophisticated, western, backed by the patchwork quilt her mother made, behind it the opening to the stable. Caught up by the overwhelming euphoria of home-coming, she greets everyone in a rich deep voice.

And there outside is the nubile village girl, yes, nubile, all those hormones streaming into her blood at the prospect of imminent marriage are making her breasts bounce up and down under the tight shiny orange jersey from Germany. She keeps her mouth shut, it is inclined to open back over the gums and she knows it. But her eyes are deep and dark and beautiful, and she keeps those firmly cast down too.

Neziha worked in a leather fabric factory, that was where the stuff for the silver waistcoat came from, and lengths to make them all waterproof jackets of white fabric. I went to see her, smoked a German cigarette. There was Pembe sitting beside Neziha, dimmed almost to invisibility by the glowing prodigal in the Joan-of-Arc waistcoat, the prodigal who had found equality with men and the freedom to earn, who held herself proudly, her stomach slim and flat. She had her eighteen months' wages, the best part of them; the guest workers in

Germany contrive to live on very little. I stubbed out my cigarette on something that wasn't really an ashtray and apologized.

'Es macht nichts.'

An unforgettable voice, rich, deep, with a funny roughness.

Muzaffer, Feride's daughter, came in to welcome Neziha, who rose and they embraced, kissing on both cheeks. I looked into Muzaffer's eyes, over Neziha's shoulders, saw something in them that was certainly not uninhibited welcome. Coldness? Thoughtfulness? I didn't know.

The family were all apparently giving Neziha a splendid welcome and she was responding with the radiance of a goddess.

By village custom, by good Nar morals, it was thought in the coffee house to be Neziha's duty to buy a bride for her brother; their mother was dead and so she, his *abla*, his elder sister, stood in a mother's place to him. She had no duty to give Pembe a dowry for Pembe was much younger, and anyhow males are always more important in village eyes.

That was certainly recognized to be her duty, but, thought the family, it would be a good thing to keep it well before her eyes, no knowing what western ideas she might have picked up in Germany. Of course Neziha would want to see the girl for herself, so they had got her over for Neziha to judge for herself what sort of bride she would make; it was not at all a question of whether she would make Ekrem happy, that could be taken for granted, a man would naturally have sex and children laid on for him as part of the natural development of his life. The only thing for Neziha to think about was whether she would fit into the family.

Müzeyen was the name of the bouncing bride.

Neziha had been very unhappily married to a Nevşehir man before she had signed on at the Labour Exchange for work in Germany. They had had a little boy called Murat; Neziha had been sending him things and had brought him presents and after a day or two of royal welcome she went in to Nevşehir to see him; he was four. Neziha herself was only twenty two, she had been married when she was sixteen.

In Nevşehir the mother-in-law whisked the child away from his mother, Neziha hardly saw him; then she herself was turned away from the house.

I went in that same evening and she was lying on the bed, paralysed with weeping, raving about whores and sons of whores. Suddenly her mood would change and she'd laugh hysterically. Three women sat round attempting to comfort her, poor bodies in faded patched *dimi*, made originally from misprint ends bought cheap in the market. One of them had a sweet smile and was only about forty but stone deaf, she looked a crone of eighty or so. She was good, I had seen her before helping Granny across the yard to the lavatory when she was too stiff with rheumatism to walk unaided. Another looked old, too, though she was about the same age; she had a child with her, a ten-year-old girl whose whiskery plaits probably hadn't been combed for a month. Another sat by Neziha's head on the bed. I thought she was old as well, but when she turned she had the face of a girl no older than Neziha herself.

Old Granny on her own bed looked wonderfully rejuvenated; she had on a new brown print dress with the brown cardigan, and some very smart patterned stockings in shades of brown. She looked quite lively, her expression almost young, but there on her quilt lay her bony, frail, heavily-veined hand. Was she rejoicing because she was childless and Neziha had lost her child? Anyhow she wasn't sympathetic to her trouble. She probably quite practically didn't want Neziha to give her own child any of her money.

I myself sat on the floor by the wall that evening, and I could see Neziha's feet swinging to emphasize a point in her tirade. She had long slender straight toes, even toenails, high insteps, and her creamy pale feet were spotlessly clean. I didn't then understand the villagers and I wanted to help her but I didn't understand her position. I felt very unhappy.

'Oh God, I only saw him for a tiny minute, I shall never see my boy again, my little boy . . . oh my boy, my boy . . .'

I went up next day and talked to Pembe's friend, Melahat, about Neziha; she had been Melahat's friend before she went away to Germany.

As far as I could understand they were asking ten thousand lira for the girl, Ekrem's affianced. Nar people don't sell their daughters but they were villagers from the outback; ten thousand lira was something like three hundred pounds and surely wouldn't leave much of Neziha's savings. But according to them, ten thousand lira would cover the cost of her upbringing and the household furnishings and compensate her father for the loss of her labour. Indeed the young girls themselves pride themselves on the high prices given for them. They look down and shyly brag about it. The girl wouldn't have a luxurious life anyhow, she would have to work hard and bear and bring up children and have very little consideration from anyone. It was easy to get angry about Pembe being disregarded and Neziha shamefully exploited, but the wretched bride would have a tough time too.

And Neziha did really want to set up her young brother in his family life; given the society in which they lived, that can be seen as a worthwhile motive, to be respected anywhere. Everyone else seemed a little too practical, too grasping.

The young couple would have a chance of proving themselves honest and fertile and brave and sensible about earning money and saving it; if they did all those things, or even some of them, they would find themselves before they died in a position of great respect in the village. Neziha was giving them that chance. It would be wonderful to have a fine old village wedding on her month's holiday. So things went on; Melahat sewed busily at German materials for dresses for the bride.

But Melahat was busy sewing for another wedding which had been looked forward to for months, quite a different sort of wedding.

I had never got to know Nesrin the teacher very well, she was a quiet girl and very busy with her responsibilities at school. Only at the school sports in May I had sat with her and Naim Bey, her fiancé, the slender young science master. I hadn't said much, because the boys were so good in their gym display I had been speechless, they were like an army team, and the four or five girls who had been allowed to do a little routine of movements, no vaulting-horse or anything like that, had been so hampered by their white pyjamas and other heavy clothes that really they had been very weak, but I applauded their

courage. Even if it was done badly, the marvellous thing in a con-
servative Muslim village was that it was done at all. So I clapped the
girls much more than the boys, but my Turkish was then too weak to
explain my complicated motives to the intelligent pair beside me. I
liked and admired them both very much, I thought their honesty and
conscientiousness stood out for all to see.

I had been giving her brother some help with his English and I had
more chance of talking to Nesrin in their house. She said she had been
to the Education Institute in Samsun; it had been a two-year course
then for secondary school teachers, lengthened to three years now, she
told me. Turkish language and literature had been her subject; she
knew something about Shakespeare, they had read *Othello*. I asked
her how she liked it and she said very honestly and simply that she
didn't remember much about it. There is a weekly called *Hayat*, Life,
a colour magazine with good and informative articles, something
like our colour supplements, and a whole pile of them had been
bound together and placed under the coffee table. She was very quiet
and didn't want to talk; I liked her very much. Her chief concern
was with people and the administrative side; it was weighing on her
and naturally she couldn't talk to me about that. Naim Bey had been
at another Education Institute in the west of Turkey. Samsun is in the
north, on the Black Sea coast. She showed me a photo of herself at the
Institute, queuing at the canteen with one of those American partitioned
food-trays in her hands. I said I very much admired the great Turkish
mystic poet Yunus Emre and had wanted to translate some of his poems
into English, but their simplicity made it difficult. She said he was
recognised as the great poet of the country and was taught in all the
schools. He was easier she thought for Turkish children to read than
Shakespeare could be for English children. He lived in the Middle
Ages and wrote about his burning love of God.

Nesrin, I knew, said her prayers regularly and kept the fast, yet she
was a capable administrator. She dressed very simply like a high school
teacher in the West, was bare-headed and never veiled herself or wore
dimi, yet she ruled her life by a strict moral code. She had resolved
in herself the conflict between the old religion and the new ideal of
womanhood.

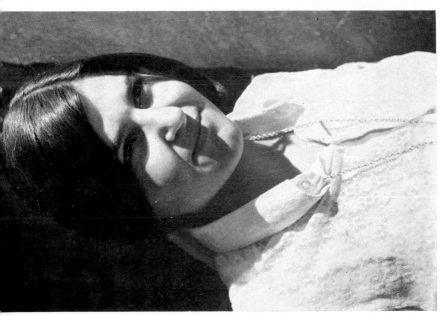

8. Pembe. 'She appeared thoughtful and sensible, a real person'

9. (*far right*) 'Granny . . . said her rheumatism was very bad'

10. The Bride.
'...under the arches of my kitchen'

I was sitting in Melahat's workroom talking about Pembe and her family; on a line hung various dresses ready for trying on. Nesrin came in for a fitting.

Naim had bought the material, a white lace, for her wedding gown in Ankara. It had to have a shiny silk lining. It was waiting for her, but another dress was put over her head first, an orange terylene that Naim had chosen specially for her. It looked terrific; she was lit up by it, it was completely different from the dark skirts and cardigans she wore for work; I think she chose them to make her look older for her responsible position. It was wonderful, that orange, she looked . . . oh, with her dark olive skin, her long nose, her pointed chin, her eyes with a hint of Mongol in their shape . . . she was flame-like. It was a plain shirt shape.

Melahat lifted it carefully off for the hem to be done up and the wedding dress was put on and shaken down into place. She stood very straight and withdrew herself completely and shyly from the onlookers. It was sleeveless and the unturned-up hem splayed out over the floor like a train. She turned obediently when Melahat asked her to but she wasn't thinking about us at all.

It wasn't until the day fixed for the wedding that her brother brought me an invitation, in the form of a folded card with a mauve posy on the front. Inside the date, the time, half-past eight in the evening, the invitation from the two families, and at the bottom the names of the two fathers, a normal, correct Turkish wedding invitation.

Melahat I know wanted to go to see the dress, apart from reasons of friendship, but when I went round to go with her she said that her husband wouldn't send her, wouldn't allow her to go. She begged me to take her little girl because she had promised her she should go, and now she was in a fix. I said of course and, putting my feelings about her husband on one side, made up my mind to make it a happy evening for little Yeşim.

We crossed the dark Meydan hand in hand and met my young friend Münevver on holiday from her biology course at the medical university in Ankara. She looked fine in a neatly-tailored pale blue dress. I had only a navy silk and wished I had brought a dress-up dress for weddings; I made up my mind to get some stuff for Melahat to make me one; she was a very good dressmaker. We sat with Münevver and her young sister by a table at the side of the room, the rather select tea-house favoured by the teachers. Nesrin's brothers, three or four of them, were of course there for the wedding and they had spent all day decorating the room with streamers and coloured lights.

They had got a guitar group with electronic equipment; it was the one the lycée students had got together. They were moving about fixing up wires and things, then Nesrin's mother and Naim's mother came in and sat in the middle in armchairs. Nesrin's mother looked pale; not long before I had called at their house and she had looked very tired, her dress and head-veil clinging to her in the heat. She had had about thirty relatives staying in the house and I don't know how she managed to feed them all. The sleeping is easy in Turkish houses, mattresses and quilts are spread on the floor and if there aren't enough you borrow. Now Nesrin's mother was transformed, bareheaded, her wavy grey hair neatly done, and the saxe-blue dress Melahat had made set off her fair complexion. She was dignified and content, the ideal mother.

Nesrin came in, wearing the long lace dress with a red ribbon round the waist, her face covered by a white veil. She sat at a table in the middle with Naim beside her. They went through the simple registration ceremony seated at the table, the signing of the book, and then listened to a short speech by the registrar wishing them well.

Naim Bey then turned to his new wife, lifted the veil from her face and laid it back over her coronet of white flowers. They spoke together quietly for a minute or two and then got up and began to dance together to the band, a simple foxtrot. Other couples joined them, filling the open space in the middle of the room.

A party had come from Naim's village in the south near Antalya, nearly six hundred kilometres away; his father, a thin, bony farmer, got up and led some of them very vigorously in a *halay*, the dance the men had done at Ortahisar; he waved his arms widely and pranced splendidly. He was brown and weather-beaten; his wife was in a veil, a little home body.

After the dancing the bride and groom came round and greeted all of us, Naim kissing all his new men relatives on both cheeks.

Nesrin went up to her father, so plainly a gentle and thoughtful person, gentle and thoughtful not from timidity but from a real respect for people. She kissed his hand and then kissed him on both cheeks. They were proud and sincere.

It was a good wedding. As well as dedicating themselves to each other they were pledging themselves to work together for Turkey. It worked out very well too. That autumn they both got jobs at a big school on the outskirts of Kayseri; a year or two later I found them there having lunch in the large, airy staffroom and shared their spicy meat *pides* and salad. I talked with the other teachers, open, intelligent men and women. The boys and girls, too, were delightfully frank and co-operative. Naim sent a girl to get more salad; she was rather a long time and when she finally arrived with it:

'Hello, have you been on the Pilgrimage?'

Nesrin was seven months pregnant then. After school Naim Bey would go and do the marketing while Nesrin went home, did all the housework and prepared an evening meal for the three of them; the younger brother who had been the excuse for the bad letter to Pembe's father was living with them and going to the Kayseri lycée. His household chore was to light the stoves when he came in from school, and to keep the house warm. Winters are cold in Kayseri and that year the night temperatures had dropped to thirty below zero. They had put their names down for a centrally-heated flat in a new block being built; the rent there would be twice as much and take perhaps a quarter of their combined salary.

I stayed the night with them very happily and next morning, when the sunlight slanted over the snowy cone of Erciyas Dag, I took some photographs. From their flat I could see over low-lying pasture to the small town where Nesrin had grown up, but both from their flat and the school it was the mountain, thirteen thousand feet high, that dominated the view. Dominated . . . that isn't quite right, one's eyes were irresistibly and pleasurably led to the snowy summit. Satisfying to look at, for the pure cone went up into light, exciting because it symbolized the drive towards education that was the purpose of the school.

14

EKREM'S WEDDING

Pembe had not gone to Nesrin's wedding, though as her dear Nesrin was her Assistant Head I had expected to see her there; Nesrin too was disappointed that she was not there. It must have been part of the letter trouble, Pembe was afraid of seeing Nesrin's brother, of being again spoken to by him. Polite refuge was taken in the very stiff formal rule, that when a whole family receives an invitation only two members of it may properly accept. I had seen Neziha and her father at the wedding, sitting quietly in a corner; I didn't speak to them.

Ekrem was to be married to Müzeyen during the last week of Neziha's stay in Turkey, and it was to be a real village wedding, with only the sound of the drums for invitation. Haci Baba's daughters were with me when they started up one Monday, and we went up to my roof and over to the other side to look.

Immediately below our feet we could look down on Haci Zelha's courtyard; I never crossed to that side of the roof on my usual business of drying clothes or shaking carpets because it would have been invading their privacy. Beyond their sheds and their chicken house was the mulberry grove, the property of the other branch of the Hacilar clan, Pembe's lot. On the bare earth beneath the trees the musicians were playing. Green leaves obscured our view and the dazzle of sun and shade camouflaged the drummer and piper. There were not many there, just a few youths in the red shirts fashionable that year, dancing in line. The sound was alluring and I thought I'd go down and get a closer look; the girls hoped their mothers might take them later in the week.

The youths in a row were dancing a *halay*. Some groups of heavily-veiled women were watching from lane-ends and corners, but none were in the grove near the dancers. Memduh Akgül's grandson came and asked me to sit in one of the chairs the musicians were using, but I said I had better not, I went against village custom even to watch from where I stood. He looked fine, his red shirt was lace. He said Müzeyen was indoors preparing a salad for the musicians' lunch. I found relatives had come from Germany and were installed on the top floor, which had been cleaned and whitewashed and laid with carpets; red curtains hung at the windows. The house was so tall that the windows commanded a wide view of the dark cliffs which rose from the willows and the walnut groves; here and there could be seen the glitter of the stream which made the valley green.

But the old cave room where Ahmet had died had not been whitewashed, not yet, the weather had been too hot, they said. That was to be the room for Ekrem and Müzeyen, the nuptial chamber. Her furniture which had all been bought with Neziha's money was stacked up in a storeroom at the back of the family house. Armchairs, a buffet, carpets in the bright colours villagers like, heaps of cushions, stacks of mattresses, a brass bedstead, all among piles of potatoes and sacks of wheat. Müzeyen was feeling fine, she had been to Nevşehir in a pretty pinkish-orange two-piece which had come from Germany, and had shown herself off in Nar; Melahat had made her more dresses. She still remained a villager, with a soft and shapeless body; she refused to wear her bras which were folded away in cases with all the other underwear and rolls of material that had been bought. Melahat tried to get her to wear them, saying she didn't know how to fit a blancmange, but she seemed to think them rather wicked. She was very sweet, actually, and as it were taken aback by her new grandeur, as though she couldn't quite believe it. She was quiet, she never spoke much.

Ekrem was, I thought, more thrilled by the chance of driving his uncle's German car than by his imminent wedding. He often went into Nevşehir and he gave me a lift once, he was very proud of himself and he was quite a good driver. For a time the poor branch of the Hacılar clan was poor no more, but the centre of life in our quarter, with its continual comings and goings, and the big Rekord being cleaned in the street. A brown car, shining. Pembe was reserved, polite if she was addressed, doing pleasantly whatever was required of her. Granny sat looking satisfied with the social life, being gracious to guests.

I stood in the shade on Tuesday, watching the slow movements of the men circling in the *halay*; little boys were scrambling up the mulberry trees and one was sprinkling water from a jar to lay the dust.

The dancers stopped, went to the chairs with bold male strides, proud. Two of them put on ankle-length full skirts with frills round the hips. One pink, one blue, checked; I recognized the stuff Neziha had said she was going to make into *köçek* skirts. An olive-skinned lad with sideboards wore the pink; he stood tying iron castanets to the fingers of each hand, fiddling with them, getting them firm. The drum and flute were put away and two men took fiddle and guitar and seated themselves, making sure they were in tune. They started up slowly and the dancers too began even more slowly, tentatively, warming up, stamping and clashing their castanets, hips and buttocks twitching. Pink Skirt began to twirl, faster and faster and faster, fingers daintily clashing. Faster and faster and faster. A wailing gipsy song had started. The lad threw back his head with a crazy laugh and went into a sort of Spanish step on his heels with his chin turned sharply to one side, over his shoulder, the whole upper part of his body possessed by the shaking motion which had started at the hips. He seemed tireless, though the sweat ran down his face in the heat of the day. Possessed, that was it, in the green shade.

Only men were in the mulberry grove; the veiled women, the neighbours, watched from the shadows of houses.

The women danced that evening in the rock room where the old man had died. It was bare of furniture, at first cooler than the air outside but the crowd of women soon warmed it. The colours they wore were gaudy; many were there from the outback village Pembe's father and the bride herself had come from. The bride's mother was in an orange blouse from Germany, dancing opposite a woman in a tight green velvet bodice above her full trousers. They danced with wooden spoons as castanets, two in each hand, ordinary wooden spoons used for soups and puddings as well as dancing. Some are painted with flowers, some with pictures of Konya and the shrine of the Mevlana, the medieval mystic who founded the sect of the Whirling Dervishes there.

There was a little woman from Adana watching, a relative who looked exactly like the busts of Roman matrons. Why not? Adana was a Roman city. The others tried to get her to dance but she squeaked in protest, saying that she never never showed her legs, she couldn't possibly take off her full *şalvar* trousers. In the end she did, turning and doing the really loud click of the fingers with both hands together, loud like a pistol shot, done somehow with the index and middle fingers.

They danced in couples, turning and wheeling back to back, clicking their spoons, shaking their breasts, swaying their hips, all in strict time with the ceaseless beating of the *def*. One short step and then the other foot shuffled up. The dancing was so ancient, so unchanging, that I found it soothing and refreshing. For how many thousands of years had the village women danced so for weddings?

I asked one or two what the dancing was for, to see what they said. I knew that no woman is considered to be properly married without it, it is more important—more ancient?—than either the civil registration or the religious ceremony.

One said she thought of love-making when she danced. Another that it had nothing at all to do with sex, it was an expression of all the happiness of being alive, ecstatic joy. Another that it was to cheer up the bride who must leave her mother and her family to go and live among strangers.

It is being replaced now by the modern western type of ballroom dancing that Nesrin had had at her wedding. No men are allowed to see the old dancing, but it is slow and dignified, except for the occasional shake of the breasts. The bride kisses the dancers' hands to thank them, but only dances herself for some special reason. Hand-kissing is difficult because a woman must only kiss the hands of someone older than herself; if two women are of more or less the same age-group they exchange a peck on both cheeks. So when a dancer had finished her dance and looked round she would only kiss the hands of women older than herself. I tried to kiss Granny's hand but she was embarrassed and wouldn't let me, but I counted it a great honour much later when I was leaving the village that Memduh's grandmother held out her hand openly for me to kiss. I liked having my own hand kissed. A lovely greeting between older women is when all four hands are clasped together and both women say a prayer.

But back to Ekrem's wedding, where they danced in the cave room till late on the Tuesday night.

The next evening would be the henna evening, when the bride's fingers and toes would have henna paste put on them and all the other women could henna their palms if they wanted to, to share in the joy and fertility which is the real meaning of the wedding.

Crowds were there on Wednesday, in the courtyard where the *def*-player was seated. News must have gone all over the village that it was being a good wedding. The Dede family was a much respected one, though Pembe's father was only *evlad*, adopted. Women were sitting everywhere, on *kilims* spread on piles of firewood or on the old cart; the stairs winding up the side of the house were a grandstand. There was a triple ring of chairs with boards put between them. Privacy was given to the dancers by an overhanging balcony, a sort of gallery, part of the area used by the father and stepmother; they couldn't be overlooked from above, where the men were feasting.

I found a perch high in a corner on some vine prunings where I hoped no one would see me. But Neziha came along and dragged me out; she was the hostess, organizing all the food and the women's side of the wedding.

'Come on up to the men's room,' she said. 'A German tourist woman is up there.'

Neziha was evidently worried and I followed her up to the door of the room on the top floor where the men were eating some delicious looking food and watching the *köçek* dancers put on their show. A blonde German woman was sitting on the floor with a towel that someone had spread modestly over her bare knees. I sat down beside her and tried to remember a few German words. She knew no Turkish; she had come with her husband who was getting on quite well with the men, standing up and gesticulating.

Then the food tray was taken away and the two boys, Pink Skirt and Blue Skirt, began to dance in earnest.

We were so close to them in the tiny stuffy room that we could see the separate beads of sweat running down their faces and hear their panting breaths. Their faces we saw in sharp perspective from where we sat on the floor. Pink Skirt bent back and back with his castanets like little cymbals clashing rhythmically all the time till he could pick up a five-lira note from the floor with his teeth and then, dancing all the time, return to an upright stance. They had been doing that all the week and appeared as fresh as ever. We were so close we could have touched a twitching sweating leg by lifting a hand. Yet it was serious, no mere cabaret turn. It was a sort of worship-prayer to the powers of nature for the life of man to go on in the village.

The blonde woman and I looked at each other and decided it was time for us to go down and join the women.

Down in the yard Müzeyen the bride was sitting in the white lace dress Neziha had made, it wasn't worth paying a dressmaker for a dress that would only be worn once. We all danced for her, the German with western vigour and lots of hip wiggles, very extrovert, quite different from the dreamy absorbed dancing of the Turks. But it was very much appreciated and applauded with '*Eline sağlik*', health to your hand. They made me dance too, time and time again, and I got into the swing of it and went home to bed feeling as though flowers must be growing out of my ears.

The next day, Thursday, was the day to fetch the bride. Of course she had already been living there for some time with her mother so it had been decided to have a ride around somewhere in cars and minibuses to give Neziha and anyone who stopped to help her time to get the bridal chamber ready and all the furniture and embroideries set out in it. Pembe's uncle, the policeman from Ankara, was there, and his wife Zeynep, the daughter of Salim Hoca. They were capable and willing people who would see everything was done well.

Our merrymaking cortège set out. There were various ideas about where we were going but no one knew except the leaders. The flute and drum played in the truck, the cars sounded their horns ceaselessly and our minibus proved to have had a past career as an ambulance, and the bell did splendidly. The bride was enthroned in the smartest of the cars, cleaned up specially and shining brightly. All three cars had

German registrations. Workmen on holiday don't have to pay car tax but come as tourists.

We went to Uçhisar, a village favoured by French tourists, about ten kilometres away. The cars stopped in the square and the *köçek* dancers got out and put on their skirts ready to dance. The fiddler tuned up and they got going, spinning madly and clashing their fingers. A crowd of young French boys and girls joined them, making up their own steps to the music, while a French lad filmed it all from a roof.

Pink Skirt, inspired by his admiring audience, did a Cossack spin, going right down to the ground, keeping his skirt standing out horizontally round him.

When we got back to the house Ekrem took his veiled bride by the hand and led her through the yard doors. As they passed Memduh took down the Turkish flag which had been flying over the wall since Monday. They went straight through the yard and into the bridal chamber which had been prepared.

Neziha stood at the door to keep the children away for five minutes or so, then Ekrem came out, pretending to see no one, went into the little room by the stable and called for his father. The women who filled the yard would not at first let his father through to talk to Ekrem, but at last he walked quickly in, and soon brought Ekrem out with him through the yard gate, neither raising their eyes among the women.

Poor Ekrem: since he was fifteen he had not been allowed to speak to a girl, scarcely to see one. He had with his male companions imbibed or evolved the idea that the only way to think of women was with erotic intent. It must have needed all his courage to get married so publicly. He might spend the afternoon with his companions, or as cheeky Pembe said, he might find a corner to have a sleep in, he wouldn't have much time that night.

The *def*-player started up, the women formed a circle round her and the dancing began again. I danced a few slow rounds with Neziha. All the women of my landlord's family were there, sharing in the wedding, giving it their countenance and acceptance. Then the guests thinned out.

I returned in the evening, and about five o'clock, found the bride sitting enthroned in her room among her new stuffed armchairs. Someone had put in some very hard work fixing the room while we had been off at Uçhisar; the chromium-plated bed took up most of the floor space and all the cushions the bride had embroidered were ranged on it. Strings had been tied across the room to display the bead-edged veils. The glass buffet covered the corner where Pembe had pumped up the old Primus for coffee as her grandfather lay dying, where the partridge's cage had hung. I sat on one of the armchairs and the bride, ill at ease, fidgeted about, standing a bit, sitting a bit. Neziha was looking over the contents of her suitcases in the recess, wondering what to take back to Germany. She was unhappy and tired; she felt that she had been exploited, indeed I think she had. All her money had gone. She didn't want to go back to Germany, the coarse-ground coffee there was so horrid, she said.

'Why don't you get a thirty-lira coffee-mill to take back with you, to make all your guests Turkish coffee?'

'I have no money left.'

I bought her one next day; proud, she gave me in return a gilt link belt which I still have.

That wedding evening Fadime Hanım, Memduh's mother, was sitting with me when we heard the last call to prayer.

'Ekrem will be going to pray in the mosque now, Salim Hoca's mosque,' she said. 'Then he will go back to his room. Let's go and see how they are getting on.'

The two grannies were sitting in the yard, against the window of the small room. Fadime sat with them. I went on into the bridal chamber, where I found Neziha making up the bride. Heavy black mascara and eyeliner for the fine dark eyes. Fresh pink lipstick for the young full mouth, pretty when serious but exposing teeth and gums when she smiled. Careful attention to her white flower crown and its silver trailer. Her white lace dress was fine . . . but the white stockings were a little dirty and must be changed. Neziha hunted about for a clean pair and slipped them on over the henna-ed toes and tied them above the knee.

A bed had been made up on a mattress on the floor in a space between the new chairs.

'What's that for?'

'Don't you know anything?' said the anxious Neziha crisply. 'They will make love there first, then the bridegroom must leave a ten-lira note in that bed to pay for the cleaning, an aunt or someone will do it in the morning, and they will spend the rest of the night in the big bed.'

Neziha went out into the yard to fill the water-jug with fresh water from the tap and I followed her. We heard footsteps and the sound of prayers from the alleyway, and Neziha hastily put the water in the chamber and ran with Pembe into Granny's little room where they stayed hidden without putting the light on; young sisters must hide from the groom as he goes to the nuptial chamber.

The people outside stood by the door while another prayer was said, then Ekrem opened the door and came in, shutting it behind him. He came and kissed the hands of his two grannies and touched them to his forehead; then he shook my hand, I was sitting beside them. Then he kissed Fadime's hand and still in silence walked through the moonlight to the door of the bridal chamber and went in, shutting it behind him. We went home.

Neziha drove back to Germany with some relations in the little white Opel; I went on the bus to see the Trade Fair at Izmir. I saw their car from the bus, driving up past the Salt Lake, but they didn't see me waving.

I stayed a day or two only at Izmir. When I got back the village was very quiet and serious, no one looked up or spoke to me, even when I bought bread in the shop. Pembe soon came to my door.

'My uncle, my mother's brother, has been killed in a car crash, they were going up to Trabzon in the brown Rekord when a tyre blew out and threw them off the road. My uncle is dead and little Şahin his son too, the boy who was playing with us in the woods on May Day. The little girl is all right but Granny Ayşe is very bad, it's her back, and my uncle's wife has broken her legs and cut herself.'

Pembe was quiet. I couldn't really take it in.

'Where are they?'

'My uncle's wife wouldn't stay in the hospital up there, she didn't want her leg put in plaster, she came back to Granny Ayşe's house for a village woman to do a cure on her leg. They are both lying in bed there now, let's go and see them.'

At the house we found Pembe's aunt (who was Fatma Defci's daughter) sitting on a bed groaning, holding her left knee. It was purple and swollen and misshapen, and cuts by the knee and on the thigh were held together by metal clips. Sometimes she was forced to move, then she screamed with pain. Granny Ayşe lay on the window seat behind her, still, with closed eyes.

'Why in God's name didn't she stay at the hospital and have the leg seen to properly?' I asked.

'You can't walk for four months when the hospital put your leg in plaster,' they told me. 'This way, she will be cured in three weeks.'

The woman healer came in with her attendant. Two ordinary women heavily wrapped in shawls and *dimi*. The healer asked for ten eggs and she separated the whites and whipped them to a stiff froth. She grated a long bar of soap and mixed it with the meringue till it was all a huge stiff mass. When she had felt the broken leg she assured us and the patient, who was groaning, that the break was one clean one and that the bones lay well together and would mend. She spread the white soap meringue on some muslin headveils and wrapped them round the leg, then made it all tight with some bandages the hospital had used. That was that. She had finished. The woman on the bed was crying and groaning all the time but in her place I would have welcomed the physical pain to take my mind off the death of husband and son . . . little Şahin, who had played in the woods on May Day.

I was told that the egg and soap was sometimes successful. But not that time, there were several breaks and the whole thing was smelly when the German car insurance firm said that she was to be taken to Kayseri Hospital. She had a lot of trouble with the leg and had to go to Ankara afterwards; she didn't come home for eight months.

Mugadder, Haci Zelha's daughter-in-law, came in to see me one evening. 'Mother says the accident was a judgement of God,' she said quietly, the image of a good woman, only caring about her own household. 'Those Kaygısız have been offending God.'

There was a handsome black-browed youngster who hadn't been with his parents in the car when it crashed. The loving and thoughtful

Pembe was drawn to him by pity; inquiries were tentatively made by both families with reference to a possible match. When I heard about it I was angry; the boy was very immature, was shaken by the crash and had no work and no plans. In addition he was Pembe's first cousin with a subnormal young brother. I tried to explain that first-cousin marriages could increase the likelihood of abnormality, but I was thankful when the boy went off to Germany to look for work.

First-cousin marriages are favoured in the village, they keep land together and the characters and dispositions of the couple are known to the families. They have a vague notion that abnormal children may result, but what of that, idiots are beloved of God. We had a village idiot called Halil and everyone was kind to him and he was always allowed on the minibuses without paying. But idiots and the insane often die very young. One girl had survived at the top of the village, she sat slavering with wild hair, like the wolf-children in the sociology textbooks. The bitter cold of the 1971–2 winter finished her sad existence.

Oh thank God Pembe didn't marry her cousin.

☙ 15 ☙

THE YEAR 1971

Neziha paid for Pembe to take an English course at the Middle School; she took the exam again in September and passed. She still had the social science and maths to get through for her Diploma.

Her father, worried that Pembe had been interested in her cousin, and there had been that dreadful letter from Mustafa too, began to think (influenced by stepmother?) that an early marriage had better be arranged to safeguard Pembe's virtue. I saw no reason why she should not take the two exams again at the end of the school year, in May. I said I would pay for her uniform and school books and give her some money to compensate her father for the loss of time on the land work. Her father was dithering and I hoped to swing him by that offer. He wondered if he should marry her to a young relative, a peasant who was willing to take her without dowry. He lived close by and if she married him she could continue to look after her Granny. Granny was in favour of that plan. Who can blame her? She wanted to end her life with affectionate attention.

I talked the business over with Melahat, who was also very fond of Pembe. Melahat too thought she might be unsettled and want to marry. She knew of the son of a dentist in Nevşehir (her husband's family was a good one, well thought of in the town) who was looking for a good wife. Inquiries were begun on both sides. Pembe's father came out with a firm 'No.' He thought the well-to-do dentist's family would look down on dowerless Pembe, with poor relations and a grandfather in jail. He was a proud man, and Pembe was a good girl, and it would not do.

I spoke to Pembe, feeling myself that what had shaken her had been her father and the gun, and the best thing for her would be to take her Diploma. It would help her to get over that experience. I said I would give her money for her dowry or her school things, whichever she herself most wanted. Probably, I said, a prospective bridegroom would respect her more if she had that Diploma. (I knew she would respect herself which was more important.) She agreed, also indirectly, saying that her sister Neziha had written from Germany that she should go on studying. So it was decided that she should do what she wanted and I bought some black nylon for Melahat to make her a new uniform.

There was a new Head at the school, Mustafa's brother-in-law had gone to do his military service. I made an appointment to take Pembe to see him. He was extremely quiet, calm and co-operative, a nice man. We sat in the little office where Harun had rented my house for me two years before and I felt as though Pembe were my own daughter. The Head soon grasped the delicate situation, we explained that her father was willing that she should try again. But, he said, he was short of desks in the school, he had put in for some but he didn't expect them before the half-year holiday in February. Perhaps it was a politic way of giving himself time to make inquiries about her family and her standard of work. It would be better if she started school in February, that was the Head's opinion. We agreed on that, shook hands, and left the office happily. The winter was slipping by, February would soon come. There was Ramazan to get through. She could study at home, revise, and be ready for school.

Of course there were many happy girls growing up in the village, girls with no family problems, brought up to blossom into womanhood in an affectionate atmosphere. Haci Baba's grandson, Mehmet, the one who had helped with cutting the grapes for the wine factory contract, had recently married such a girl; a charming, glowing round-faced child from a house at the top of the village, by the threshing-floor. We saw her a little at Haci Baba's for everyone liked her, but her husband Mehmet was away doing his military service at Alexandretta, where he was an N.C.O.

On the whole such girls, belonging to Nar, lived such full and happy lives that I hadn't much chance of getting to know them. Anyhow they were content and had no problems. One family I did know well was that of Huriye Hanım, the dear woman who had taken me on a picnic and had made me feel so enwrapped in peace that I had gone to sleep. She had four daughters; Sabiha the eldest at Teacher Training School, Nurcan and Lâle at Middle School, and a baby girl, Songül, the Last Rose, a lovely, blue-eyed little Mongol girl with the most feminine finger gestures. The father came from a Mongol village in the mountain pastures the other side of Kayseri; he had called his only boy Genghiz, so he must have been proud of his ancestry. The elder girls were noticeably nicely dressed. Huriye herself was plump, looked older than her age, ran around in old *dimis*. Sabiha was engaged to the son of a man who had come to Nar at the time of the Erzincan earthquake; he had not returned but settled down with a local girl. Neither of the families was a belonging *yerli* one, so in a sense that threw them together. They were not members of the local aristocracy. The fiancé, Mehmet, had completed his training at the Boys' Primary Teacher Training School thirty miles to the north of Nevşehir and was working at a school in Kayseri Province.

Sabiha's father, Hanefi Aslan, was lonely in Nar. He renewed a friendship with a man with whom he had trained who was teaching at Sineson, a village twenty-five kilometres to the east, and the whole family moved there to live. Huriye Hanım belonged there, she was all right, she had worthy aunts and sisters living round about to share things with her, to give her the use of land. Of course I went to see them, now living in a wonderful old Greek house. Sineson was a very romantic and ruinous village whose Greek Christian population had been sent to Greece by Atatürk, some of their empty houses had in turn been occupied by Muslims transplanted from the neighbourhood of Salonica. The people were fair and talkative, and their donkeys had saddles of a Greek pattern. Hanefi was happy and Huriye brought them loads of grapes and potatoes and beans and milk from her family lands and looked splendid now that she was so busy. Sabiha had another year to finish at the Nevşehir Teachers' School. Her fiancé came to visit and told her about the village his school was in, where he was collecting nursery rhymes and where the woods were full of scented hyacinths. I had a car again that spring, while Pembe was at school, and I took an Istanbul lady and her son to picnic near Sineson

K   145

village, out of sight of the houses in fact, but we had hardly got our kettle boiling before Huriye came running down through the flowers; she had recognized me from where she was working in her field. We embraced happily. Huriye, of course, was wearing *dimi*, bunched up and knotted in front.

'Are you pregnant?' was the Istanbul lady's first greeting to her.

I was unhappy and shocked. Huriye didn't seem to mind a bit though she became less expansive. In Turkey there seems to be a barrier between city and village women; while accepting their common femaleness, city women don't respect village women, in the way that I feel every human being is entitled to respect. But perhaps such personal questions are indeed usual conversation openers. I was used to such questions as 'How old are you?', 'Are your teeth false?' and so forth.

Anyhow, I was always made welcome at Huriye's Sineson house.

Then there was the Yilmaz family who were torn between Germany and Nar. The father had taken the two middle girls and the little boy back to Germany, leaving his wife and Memnune, the eldest daughter, who had bravely landed herself a good job in the telephone exchange. Before I came to Nar Memnune had gone to the Lycée for one year, then she had failed one exam and her father had said she could not go on there, that she wasn't industrious, wasn't trying. At the Nevşehir telephone exchange the girls worked at nights every other week and often Memnune slept there; in Ramazan of course they had the night meal there and I believe they had a lot of fun. But it was a long trudge back to Nar; Memnune's long hair and woolly overcoat was a familiar sight on the road that winter. No one looked at her, she was on known business and respected by local people. A young policeman in Nevşehir saw her and fell in love with her; her father wrote a letter from Germany saying 'Give her', and they were engaged very quietly late one night when Memnune came off work. But things were not right, his mother didn't come from the far Black Sea province where they lived, where his father was an official in the tobacco office. It was found out that he was already married. Did I say bigamy is not a crime in Turkey? So they had no case to bring to court, though even Memnune said he was a mannerless oaf and wouldn't speak of him; her father refused to give her as a second wife and the match was broken off. Memnune continued to plod to work. He had been a pleasant lad and much in love.

Then the father came home from Germany and arranged for his mother to have a cataract operation in Kayseri hospital. She was over ninety, she had had the last boy, the father, when she was nearly fifty. She wasn't very intelligent but was a friendly old soul who used to embrace me all the more fondly because she couldn't see me. The operation was successful and her son took the bandages off at the appointed time, and she regained some sight. They had tried taking her to Germany but she couldn't settle there, she was too old, she said, to make the change.

Her daughter-in-law still longed to go to Germany with her husband; she feared he would get entangled with another woman. She tried looking at herself without her headveil, to see how she would look in Germany. She was lively, with good eyes, and we decided she was beautiful, she had nothing to worry about. Her father Osman, however, did not want her to go. A quiet friendly man, one couldn't blame him; he had lost two brothers in the First World War, one after the other, and he didn't like people going away.

Just at Christmas the passport papers came through and Osman and I went to Nevşehir to see Memnune's mother off on the bus to Ankara where she would get a plane and arrive when her husband had a holiday to welcome her. Osman looked very sad and hangdog for months and months, wandering sadly up and down the street looking much older. Memnune stayed to look after her grandmother and dreamed about the family in Germany. But they came back in the summer and found a worthy young man for her in Ankara. All of them hoped to make their lives in Germany. The third girl in the family was doing well at a German technical college and was going to be an interpreter in a factory; Memnune's fiancé would join them when he had finished the course he was doing in Ankara. I had made the acquaintance of a friend of Memnune when she had been looking after her granny; a tallish girl called Hayriye, with fine bony features and laughing straightforward eyes. Hayriye married a young motor mechanic and went to live in Ankara. They took a house not far from where Pembe's uncle, the policeman, lived with his wife Zeynep, the daughter of Salim Hoca, so it was almost a little Nar colony. But Hayriye's house was in a *gecekondu* area, a squatter area with no roads or water laid on, though they did have electricity. There was a well just outside their garden, and they paid less than half the rent Zeynep and her family had to pay. Hayriye and Zeynep often visited each other and kept in touch.

I saw a lot of a younger girl called Şengül Denk; I had given her English lessons in my second Nar summer and I had got to know her mother who lived right at the top of the hill. Şengül was well built, with rosy cheeks and pleasant brown eyes. Her mother, a Nevşehir woman who had married a Nar man, was a dear, and very sensible. She was a mother to me, she taught me the Arabic prayers necessary for the *namaz* ritual, and all the movements, the standing, the bowing, the kneeling, to go with them. I found the Arabic words musical and beautiful, though they were meaningless to me. I longed to be able to worship with Şengül and her mother, to do *namaz*, but legs and ears and arms had to be washed in the proper order and I always forgot it. Really no more than putting on tidy clothes to go to church; it is only a matter of what you are used to.

Behind their house, between it and the actual top of the rock of Nar, they had a little garden, with roses and dahlias and a crimson-spiked castor oil plant. A baby hedgehog lived in it. He had no special name but was called simply 'Kirpi', hedgehog. He was a family pet, Şengül's brother had found him down among the gardens in the valley bottom. I took him in the hollow of my hand and he immediately curled up and went to sleep. His whiskers were singed where he had walked into the fire, for he was totally without fear of anything. He was so young that his spines were still soft, banded with dark stripes. I know English hedgehogs have the name of being flea-ridden, but Kirpi didn't have one single flea, I looked in all the soft hairy patches under his armpits and by his legs. He ate insects and flies, he didn't mind in the least if the flies had been poisoned, and he drank milk. I am afraid they planned to eat him when he was big and fat, but they didn't really build on doing so for they offered him to me as a pet. I couldn't take him because he could not have entered England. I am glad to say he ran away one day and I hope he is still catching flies in some pleasant Nar vineyard.

Şengül got her Middle School Diploma at the end of the year and took a place in the Girls' Craft School in Nevşehir, where she would train to take needlework classes in the villages. Pembe had failed the maths again, she told me, shy with disappointment, but she had passed the social science. 'Cheer up,' I said, 'There is a course in Nevşehir, that will be fun, take it in September. Here's the money.' Sabiha too had failed one or two finals but she was going ahead with her marriage plans; she too would take the exams again in September. Her wedding was to be at Sineson, then they would come back to a room in Mehmet's parents' house in Nar, and they hoped to get a teaching job at the same school, together, in September.

Pembe was cheerful; she was living with her Granny Ayşe, who was good company. She had recovered from the back injury she had suffered in the car crash, but she had given up all her out-of-doors work and sold her cow. Pembe's other Granny had left the little room we had spring-cleaned when Ekrem had gone to do his military service, and was living in Ekrem's mother-in-law's house, almost next door, where she had her bed by a sunny window and she could look out at passers-by through the green leaves of a hanging vine. She had got sunshine, but she hadn't got Pembe and missed her sincerity and thoughtfulness. The standards of the villagers around her were not her standards. What had happened to the young bride who had come to the tall house hoping to fill it with children? Things were hopelessly wrong. 'Çingene çalar, Kürd oynar,' she said, 'The gipsy plays, the Kurd dances.' Meaningless activities went on around her, she wanted nothing more to do with the world.

Pembe and Fadime went with me to Sabiha's wedding at Sineson; we took Fatma Defci to play for the dancing. The magnificent architecture of the old Greek houses lent space and ceremony to the proceedings. Arches, courts, balconies, were often ruinous but disguised by a tumble of pink geraniums or oleanders tended by the flower-loving Turks. The wedding house at the top of a steep lane was not the least splendid; Huriye Hanım had colour-washed one side of it a deep pink, and the other, where the carved doorway was, a bright yellow ochre. On either side of the inner court were kitchens where women were preparing food for the many guests.

We sat in a high barrel-vaulted pink-washed room to watch the dancing. Sabiha's grandmother from the village in the mountain pastures beyond Kayseri had an unveiled face of Mongol type, framed by an embroidered yellow headscarf. Her two daughters were slant-eyed neat women, who would take Sabiha to her new home to bear witness to her virginity. The rosy light from the walls was reflected from the gold coins swinging on the dancers' breasts. A girl in pink danced with bent head, using wooden spoons as castanets. Fadime danced. I danced. Sabiha bent blushing to kiss our hands. The exciting thing about the dancing was that it was not a show, the women were putting their heart and soul into it and were not being self-conscious. Two gold-hung women jumped opposite each other with much dignity in a dance called *kayalar*, 'the rocks'. They leapt from side to side, each kicking up her feet to touch the other's.

The dancers that day were not as carefree as they had been at the *pazarlık* in the spring, a party given by the bride's family so that all the gifts and equipment and dowry can be closely inspected by every-one, at which a dressmaker cuts out a dress and nightdress and takes them home to make up. All the women dance happily at a *pazarlık*, for there are no worries and no sadness, as at a wedding when a beloved girl is leaving home.

On the wedding afternoon Fatma Defci played in a sunny court-yard where many women and young girl visitors danced below a Greek pediment; Pembe in a flowered tunic with a beaded pendant her grandfather in prison had made swinging from her neck, another girl in a pleated petunia-coloured dress, another in gold lurex who was clicking her fingers loudly. Fatma banged away vigorously in the shade and some little boys watched from behind bushes, presumably assessing any qualities the little girls might have as future brides.

Meanwhile, all the bride's gear was being packed on a truck to go to Nar, where the honeymoon was to be spent. Piles of yellow cushions came out, and mattresses in gaudy covers, and a buffet and a bed. Then it left with every space filled by male friends for the unloading.

Her sisters helped Sabiha to get ready, putting the last touches to her attire by throwing a red transparent veil over her head. Then she cried, her eyes were downcast and we could see the big tear-drops running down her face even under the veil as her bridegroom led her down the steps to a waiting taxi. Huriye Hanım, the bride's mother, had hidden herself, sad too. We bundled into cars and taxis and got back to Nar in time to see the sacrifice. A sheep's throat was cut on the threshold of the nuptial house, and bride and groom stepped over the blood on the way in. Memduh, the same handsome Memduh in a bright red shirt, the acknowledged leader of the unmarried youths at that time, had some friends on the roof to take down the flag displayed during weddings, and joyfully fired off his gun several times, standing up there in the brilliant sunshine.

Mehmet and Sabiha talked and prayed a while, then I was asked in to see their rooms. They were to stay there until the end of the school holidays, when they hoped Sabiha would have finished her exams and they could get teaching posts in the same village, wherever it might be. The rooms were part of Mehmet's parents' house; a balcony over-looked the swiftly-running brook and was overhung by green willows. On one side of the balcony was their sitting-room, complete with armchairs and wall tapestries, and on the other their bedroom, with a little kitchen-space and a low sink for bathing at the back in a tiny antechamber. All Sabiha's embroideries had been arranged in the bedroom, the cushions piled on the bed and headveils with the other pretty things she had made put over cords strung across the room for their display.

I didn't see much of them until September, when Sabiha had finished her exams and got a posting to a village in Kayseri province. Mehmet had been teaching miles away, in the south of the province while Sabiha's village of Persek was to the north-east, and came under the Town Governor of Tomarza, fifty kilometres east of Kayseri. They very much wanted to be together, and it is the policy of the Education Ministry to give married couples jobs in the same place. In Turkey jobs are very much a personal matter—and why not? Who did they know who would help? They didn't, but I did. Harun, who had helped me to get a residence permit and a house when I first arrived, had finished his military service and been posted as Town

Governor of Tomarza. I went to see him, to wish him luck in his new appointment, and he asked me if there was anything he could do for me. 'No,' I said vaguely. 'Where is Persek? My friend Sabiha has just got a job teaching there. She doesn't want to be there because her husband teaches a long way away in the south of the province.'

'That won't do,' said Harun. 'Of course they must be together. Persek is one of my villages. I am going to see the Province Governor in Kayseri this afternoon and will ask him about it.'

It all worked out wonderfully; Harun got them a job together in his area, and it had a teacher's lodging, and Sabiha taught the first-year children, the seven-year-olds, and they were very happy. Harun saw it, rightly, as part of a Governor's responsibility, whether in province or town, to have people doing their work to the best of their ability and to get them what facilities they wanted for doing it. (I have used 'Town Governor' as the translation of *Kaymakam* and 'Province Governor' as the translation of *Vali*—see the Note on Local Government.)

That winter I spent a day with Sabiha and Mehmet at her mother's house in Sineson, and they were obviously happy. The ruinous hilly village was deep in snow and we walked round admiring it and snow-balling each other. Huriye gave me a bed in a little side-room where a fire had been lit and the window close-sealed against the cold; I sank deep into sleep in the peaceful house just as I had done on Huriye's picnic. For breakfast there was clotted cream; a dish of it was set on a low table-board, and we broke our bread, taking turns to dip a piece into the cream.

That summer Melahat the dressmaker was unhappy. Her husband had bought some very expensive tumbler pigeons and converted a rock chamber above their main dwelling into a pigeon house; he had whitewashed it and prepared it with great care, and spent much of his time feeding the birds and watching their lovely tumbling flight in the air above the mosque and the valley. He cared for his two dogs, too, and took them on long shooting expeditions. His own house needed painting very badly and he grudged the food the children ate, even though it had been bought with Melahat's earnings. Though he was thirty, he was nothing but an irresponsible boy.

At last Melahat's uncle decided it must not go on and came down in a car and fetched Melahat and her daughter Yeşim to his house in Ankara. Her little son was at the husband's mother's, where he stayed. Melahat and her husband had often told me they wanted a divorce, if only they could find a home for little Yeşim, who was disliked by her grandmother. It was in fact a block of flats belonging to several of her uncles that Melahat went to; I visited her there and was astonished at her transformation from an unhappy villager in old *dimi* to a neat young townswoman; she was only twenty-four. But she was still unsettled and sad.

The basement flat in the block, with the lowest rent, might soon be vacated; it would be a good place for her to start up a dressmaking business. Meantime we decided to go up to the province of Trebizond, where her people came from, for a holiday. I had a car then and so we drove there; Yeşim was good and slept most of the way. We paddled in the Black Sea, looked at the fine paintings in the Sofia church in Trebizond, and reached a relative's farm at dusk. Next day we went on up a muddy road straight into the mountains to a village called Horhor. A boy led us up a steep footpath to their old family house. It was empty now for most of the year, all the sons had good posts in Ankara or Izmir or Istanbul where they were rich and established, but Melahat's Granny and an aunt were there harvesting hazelnuts, and we helped. The damp air was refreshing after the August heat of the arid plateau; blue willow gentians and golden elecampane grew wild round the old house which was built of enormously thick oak planks.

I woke at night to woodland sounds: jackals howling and a mouse playing football with a hazel nut in the attic. Granny had told us a story.

'It was when I was a girl about Yeşim's age. There was an old woman living alone up there, and one evening two strange people came to her door, all covered with long hair. The good woman naturally offered them hospitality; she had cooked some soup and was eating it with a spoon. The two hairy people, a man and a woman, took spoons too and drank the soup as they saw her doing, though they didn't speak. The next night, too, they copied her every movement.

But the next night she felt a little bored, the correct period for Muslim hospitality had passed. As they sat to supper, she took a log of wood from beside the fire and put it down the bosom of her dress. The hairy man and the hairy woman also took logs, the only ones by the fire, which were burning at one end. They thrust them into the long hair covering them and rushed from the door with flames streaming behind them. The old woman never saw them again.

'Yes, it really happened, just across there.'

Another night before we went to bed we heard the muezzin calling a long, long *selah* from the minaret across the steep-sided valley. On and on it went, echoing sadly. Then the gunfire started up; every man in the valley must have used up all his ammunition and each shot echoed and re-echoed till we couldn't tell where any of them were coming from.

'Oh,' said Melahat, 'it's the eclipse of the moon. They are lamenting her loss, and shooting to bring her back.'

She accepted it as quite natural.

We went down to see her other grandparents in the low, warm part of the valley, not far from the sea. Maize and tea were grown everywhere. The tea had been harvested in May and again in June; now in August the leaves on the little tea bushes were dark green and tough. After they had given us tea in a sunny room they showed us the hazel nuts which had been laid out to dry in the yard until they fell away from their green cups; then we crossed the road to visit the old maize mill where meal, a staple of the diet in that region, is ground. Their family were all away studying or had fitted into city life and only came to visit them in the summer.

Melahat helped her grandmother with the nut-gathering and then went back to Ankara to do some dressmaking for her uncles' wives. The last time I saw her she had settled into the basement flat of the uncles' block and was making dresses for customers. I did what I could to help her get started, for a woman needs courage to start a business alone in Turkey. She was forced to make the attempt so that she could keep little Yeşim with her; an aunt would have taken her into her household if she had been alone. The little girl was very happy in Ankara, romping about the block of flats every day after school, a cheerful member of a crowd of little cousins. Melahat was brave and intelligent; I missed her very much when I went back to Nar.

Münevver, the biology student at Hacettepe Medical University at Ankara, the girl who had taken me to a circumcision, had managed to change from the biology course to pharmacy, a chance she had been hoping for ever since she started there. She would lose a year, and would have to take an extra one before qualifying, but she thought there was no hope of an interesting job in biology without taking an extra three-year course in micro-biology or biochemistry, so it didn't matter. She found the work difficult, but managed to pass the half-year exams successfully, to her great joy.

Pembe too passed her maths exam and got her Middle School diploma that autumn. She went to stay with her uncle and his wife Zeynep, Salim Hoca's daughter, in Ankara to try for a place in the Health School where she could qualify as a midwife. She looked radiant. The possession of that diploma had given her back her self-respect.

❧ 16 ❧

PEMBE AND İSMAİL

In 1971 Ramazan began in October; the weather was not right for sowing wheat in the first part of the month, rains had not softened the earth, so most people in Nar had to work hard at ploughing in the Holy Month of the fast. I kept the fast of course and had some wonderful *iftar*, fast-breaking meals, with my friends. I have never known such peace as in the last half-hour before the meal, watching the shadows slide up the hills until dusk possessed the whole landscape. Love-feasts, *agape* meals, must have been like that among the early Christians. Unfortunately, after ten days I went down with jaundice and I couldn't fast any more, the doctor said I must drink plenty of sweet tea and water to wash the bile from my blood, and eat grapes to provide sugar, and no fats. I felt ill and disgusted with the horrid disease, but my friend Zikriye Hanım put me to bed and looked after me, then I went down to the American College at Tarsus to convalesce. They were wonderful to me there; somehow the acceptance of their care and kindness made me very happy too, so altogether I had a good Ramazan.

When I came back into Nar from Tarsus I saw three women huddled together outside my door, shivering in brown shawls in the cold. I didn't know any of them.

'We are now come from mourning the death of Pembe's Grandmother,' they said. 'God has mercifully let her escape. Two years she lived after Ahmet's death, two years.'

They were right, her death was merciful, she had always been in pain from rheumatism. Pembe was away staying with her aunt Zeynep in Ankara, she soon came back and told me her news.

'I didn't get a place in the Health School; when I got there there were about a thousand girls trying for thirty places. I stayed on with my uncle and aunt wondering what it would be best for me to do. My uncle rents his house, he gives four hundred lira a month, so he lets the lower flat. One day I was going to the shop for my aunt when a young man, a friend of the family below, stood aside for me on the steps. He was friendly with my uncle too, they are all in the Ankara police. He is called İsmail. His elder brother is in the police in Erzurum, a city in the east. He asked my uncle for me. My father agreed to give me. We had the engagement party while you were away.'

Pembe looked happy, no longer tomboyish as she had been before the bad letter, but at peace. I trusted Zeynep's judgement and knew he must be a good man, but I longed to see him for myself.

We talked it over at Granny Ayşe's one evening with Salim Hoca's wife, a good woman with great dignity and a reserved kindness. Latife was there with her pregnant daughter; Latife was the wife of Şevket Kaygısız, Old Mehmet's son by his first wife, the one who was mentally unstable. The daughter had a toddler with her too, he ran up to his mum and patted her belly and said:

'My mum is going to do a birth, there's another baby here and I shall have a little brother.'

The house was fresh and clean, Ayşe is a fine housewife, the stove was burning brightly. There on the wall was an enlarged photo of Mahir who had been killed in the car crash.

Cases were opened and Pembe showed us her clothes; İsmail had bought the engagement dress ready-made in Ankara, it was light navy with string-coloured embroidery at the neck. She had a warm fluffy tweed coat with a buttoned back belt . . . they showed me heaps of things. There were separate piles of shirts and underlinen for each man in the groom's family, each pile wrapped in an embroidered cloth, a pink cloth, pink for Pembe. Two piles of women's underlinen, also in pink cloths. There was a pair of socks in each man's pile knitted from very finely spun wool. Pembe's mother had spun the wool and knitted the socks for Pembe's dowry before she died.

İsmail's mother had not come from Erzurum for the engagement party. They said she had rheumatism badly and Erzurum is very far away, and famous for the extreme cold of its winters. She and his father were living with the eldest son who was a police commissar there. I felt worried, remembering Memnune's young man whose mother hadn't turned up at the engagement and how he had proved to be already married. I sat and tried to forget my worries though; everyone seemed to think it would be all right. I just thought it too good to be true.

As I sat thinking and admiring the embroideries, Pembe got up and took the crochet dust-cover off a little oil lamp. Saying 'In the name of God the compassionate, the merciful', she lit it and led us out across the snowy yard to an outhouse. It had been empty but now it was full of furniture, piled up, folded carpets and stuffed chairs, mattresses and bedding.

'My things,' said Pembe proudly.

'Who paid for them?' I asked.

'Mehmet, my husband, whom we went to see in prison,' said Ayşe.

'Where did the money come from?'

'You know the Commando Barracks across the valley? Well, they wanted a vineyard of Mehmet's, in the end they gave him two thousand four hundred for it. He wanted to give all that money to Pembe for her dowry.'

So while he was sitting in prison an opportunity had come to him of playing an active part in the world, of setting up Pembe, whom he loved, in her married life. It had mattered to him, he was still alive and part of things.

Pembe and Ayşe had taken me to see him when he was still in Nevşehir prison a couple of years before. Loaded with donkey bags full of yoğurt jars and cheese and things we had got on a minibus plying to the top of the hill in Nevşehir, had sat on piles of beet, and had dismounted awkwardly near the jail. The building was an old Armenian church with a double-headed eagle carved on the pediment over the west end. Below it prisoners in ordinary clothes had been chopping up firewood with huge lethal-looking axes. Down at his office by the three apses of the east end the Governor, who happened to be Harun's uncle, had given me permission to go in.

Inside some visitors were talking to their relatives at a sort of wooden fence fixed on a counter; we waited. Presently Mehmet emerged from a passage at the side and greeted us warmly, acting the good host. He ordered tea for us and it soon came.

While Pembe and Ayşe and Mehmet squatted together in a corner talking about private business I watched the other visitors. Being in prison was no disgrace, just an awkwardness, and the atmosphere was cosy and friendly; I wondered how it could be a deterrent. No training was offered, and the prisoners didn't have to work—the ones I could glimpse through an open door were just sitting about drinking tea.

A spruce young fellow in a mustard-yellow suit led an old man up the steps and in through the door, the old man carrying two donkey-bags of provisions. They talked to a prisoner for some time through the fence, then he came round to say goodbye; he kissed them on both cheeks and bent to kiss the old man's hand. He turned to come back into the prison and I saw he was very young and that tears were running down his cheeks. I think that it is the separation from their families that is the deterrent; Turks are so intensely family-centred.

I had taken Ayşe to see Mehmet again just before they moved him to Kırşehir, forty miles away. Too far to visit easily and it seemed that Ayşe would hardly ever see him now. All the long-term prisoners had been moved there. He was very depressed, I was afraid he would cry on my shoulder. He hadn't really committed any malicious crime, had just got involved in a fight. Both of them had been wounded, but the other man had got off. Mehmet gave me a blue-beaded purse that had been made in the prison; I used it to keep my precious residence permit in.

So Mehmet had provided all those things for Pembe. I felt a stab of jealousy, I would have liked to help. Salim Hoca's wife had said Pembe would like a pressure cooker and I was going to get her one, but that wasn't much.

Back in the house Pembe showed me her gold ring with the name 'İsmail' inside. I told her she was a woman now and mustn't behave like a tomboy any more. Salim Hoca's wife backed me up, but Pembe waggled her bottom cheerily as she went out into the corridor to get something. She had eight gold bracelets on her arm.

Zeynep her aunt came down from Ankara; she it was who had got everything together, the gifts of underwear for İsmail's family and Pembe's trousseau. Like all her family she had terrific confidence, she made up her own mind what was the right thing to do and then did it. I knew her father Salim Hoca well by sight for he used to walk down the street outside on his way to read the call to prayer five times a day. He was tall, with a round face, and wore small spectacles and usually a white skull-cap. His appearance didn't inspire confidence, perhaps because of the rather fleshy face and small spectacles, but I slowly found out that he was an exceedingly good man. I would rely on him completely if I were looking for good advice. Zeynep, they told me, had seen her husband, young Mehmet Kaygısız, at school and had then and there decided that he was her man, in spite of the latent bad feeling between the Kaygısız and Kozan families. Salim Hoca was of course a grandson of Kozankızı, the formidable founder of the clan. Zeynep had really taken Pembe under her wing and was in charge of all the wedding arrangements. She was Pembe's maternal uncle's wife, a very strong character and a very good woman. Her Mehmet seemed a good man. Then there was his half-brother Şevket Kaygısız, Latife's husband. Everyone in Nevşehir liked and respected Şevket, he was a car and truck driver in Government service. Latife, too, was closely concerned with Pembe's wedding; and in Ankara Hayriye, Memnune's old friend, did all she could to help. And I. So there we were, Zeynep, Ayşe, Salim Hoca's wife (her name was Fatma but there were so many of that name, nearly as many among the women as Mehmets among the men), Latife, and myself, in that last week of the year acting as informal committee to do all we could for Pembe. For believe it or not, her father hadn't given a brass farthing towards her wedding. Her sister had promised to send money from Germany but she had had expenses, had dented someone's car or something; Pembe's money would have to wait.

They asked me if the wedding dancing could be in my downstairs area, my 'crypt'. I was thrilled at the idea, but it was the deep of winter and I only had a small oil stove to heat it a little. They said it would be all right, the women could keep warm by dancing. So I made plans to clear it, to put my gas oven upstairs and the food-safe in the cave at the back. I could do nothing about the heap of coal stored there but they said that didn't matter. To clear that space for Pembe's wedding was the most delightful thing I have ever been asked to do.

Meanwhile, in Ayşe's house across the street, Pembe went on with her embroideries and fixed up covers for the pillows. She didn't come up to see me or go to the shop as much as she had done, but tried to keep indoors like a good Muslim wife, who must never leave her husband's house unless it is necessary. She practised cooking; walnut pilau was her best dish; they had plenty of wheat and walnuts of their own growing but not much money. I know now they were in debt already over the furniture. One day Ayşe asked me to pay for a strip of passage carpet that the weaver had made from a lot of old dresses which they had cut into narrow strips and then twisted the strips into coarse yarn. They are fine, those *yolluks*, everyone uses them, and they remind women happily of when they wore the old dresses. They are very easily washable.

Then one day Ayşe remembered with horror that they hadn't got her a coffee set, six of the tiny cups and saucers in which to offer guests coffee, the absolutely necessary *ikram*, polite refreshment for guests. Ayşe and Pembe and I went in to a new shop in Nevşehir and I encouraged Pembe to choose the ones she liked. She looked at all of them, silently. I looked at her; she had changed, she wasn't like the old Pembe, she was under a spell, lost. Enchanted? She had a blue-green cup with gold twiddles in a band round the top in her hand. A man of about fifty came up to Ayşe, asked her who the bride was. He said the blue-green cups were good and she chose those. The shopkeeper wrapped them up and I paid and we went out and bought some shampoo at the chemists and went home. Ayşe had asked me to get the shampoo, it's not a thing villagers use. A girl had borrowed mine at the baths and used it and washed her hair again with soap. Ayşe was intelligent and ready to accept new ideas.

I had felt proud of Pembe in the shop. She was so honest, it was fascinating to see her grow into being a bride.

That was on a Saturday; the bridegroom was expected on the Monday, Zeynep on the Tuesday. We'd have the dancing and the henna-ing on the Wednesday and I would take them to Ankara on the Thursday, the right day of the week for the wedding night. İsmail had rented a house not far from Zeynep's and had been living in it for a month; Zeynep was planning to go round and clean it up on Monday after İsmail had left, making it ready for the furniture stored in the outhouse in Nar which would follow the bride up on a bus, with any guests that cared to come.

I went round at about five in the afternoon on Monday to see if anyone had arrived. No one had and there was no news. Akgül and one or two neighbours were sitting waiting with them. I told you how very fond Akgül was of Pembe. Suddenly everyone thrilled, stood up, went to the door. They were all coming into the yard, all of them. İsmail the bridegroom, a young cousin of his, Zeynep and Mehmet and their two little girls, the other policeman, their lodger, with his wife with two small children, Hayriye and a plump dark Nar girl with her Ankara husband and two more children.

Salim Hoca soon heard his daughter had come, and arrived himself and was given a place of honour by the window; then Şevket, Latife's husband, came in. Ayşe and Pembe went out to the kitchen where Zeynep was busy frying sausage for a meal for everyone.

Salim Hoca looked benevolent as a saint, perhaps he is one. Şevket was talking a lot as he usually does; his trouble was that the marriage registrar was still away on his New Year holidays. The marriage registration has to be in the girl's home town, it could not be in Ankara. The policemen, including the groom, had only five days' leave and couldn't stay over Thursday. Salim was quite unconcerned, perhaps they could have the registration later, in Ankara. Or if not, everyone could come down to Nar for another holiday later, another party. Of course he would himself have already tied the religious knot and the civil ceremony meant little to him. But I was worried; I wanted everything to be regular and above-board for Pembe.

Salim Hoca went home and glasses of tea were brought in. I had one and the groom came and sat at the end of the window-seat, where Salim had been, and surreptitiously looked at me and I at him. Then I looked straight at him and laughed a bit and told him how very fond I had become of Pembe, she had been so good to me since I had arrived in Nar two and a half years before. He asked me what I was doing in Nar. I said I was preparing a book which I hoped would tell

English people how people lived in Nar. I asked him what he did and he said he was a police commissar in Ankara; his father had retired from the police and was living with his elder brother in Erzurum. His mother was very old and had rheumatism badly, that was why she had not come to Nar with them. I found out afterwards, she told me indeed, that a letter informing her of the planned date had gone astray and she was very sorry not to have been given the chance to come. I wasn't surprised, I have known a letter to take a fortnight to get to Nar from Tarsus, a mere four hours' easy car drive. But İsmail had a very pleasant personality, shy yet open, and his sister's boy was there as well, so I stopped worrying about his intentions being not very serious and settled down to enjoy the wedding.

I would clean up my house ready for the dancing the next morning, the Tuesday, and we'd have the dancing that night and go to Ankara on Wednesday, to their new house. I hoped there would not be heavy snow to block the roads. I went out quickly and home to bed; there are no long goodbyes in Turkey, the formality of a visit is all at the beginning. The weather wasn't bad, there was ice on the shady side of the street and wreaths and trails of snow all over the fields and hillsides, but the asphalt roads were perfectly clear.

Next morning I prepared the crypt and swept it. I had had it limewashed in the spring and it didn't look bad. I put up a poster of soldiers in ancient costume, and a bunch of wheat and barley and rye I had saved from the harvest, tied with a gold ribbon. Not a local custom, just my own idea, but they liked it.

Over at Ayşe's they had had a wonderful morning's chat, receiving visitors all the time, and had made plans for the afternoon. Pembe was going in to get her hair done at the hairdressers in Nevşehir.

Off we went, Hayriye, Latife, Pembe and I. First we looked at the bridal gowns that were displayed for hire in a window in the new shopping arcade; Pembe liked one made of white lace with three flounces in the skirt and silver leaves sewn round the neck. Latife hired it with the groom's money.

In the hairdresser's Pembe had to decide on a style.

'Don't tell him it's for a wedding,' she whispered in the doorway, 'or he'll charge me a hundred.'

L*   163

After an hour of washing, drying and combing out, her hair looked just as she wanted it, piled in high loops on the top of her head with a long corkscrew curl down over her shoulder. We got some hair-spray so that her hair would look good next day. While Hayriye had been chaperoning Pembe, I had been trying to borrow or hire a flash for my camera. I couldn't get one; none of the photographers had one to go into the shoe on the top, but I was able to borrow a big flash apparatus complete with its own camera. This was going to be my nearest approach ever to marrying off a daughter; I was deter-mined to have a record of it.

Back in Nar it was almost dark. The others went into Ayşe's while I had a sandwich and tried to stop a few icy draughts in the crypt, then Fatma Defci came in and fixed her chair as she wanted it. Dear old Fatma, of the untidy house and the ambiguous wedding songs; no one was on good terms with her, the mischief-making old thing, and she couldn't keep up the passionate beat and the crooning songs at full pitch for long, but Nar wouldn't be the same without her. Village relationships are so complicated: Fatma's daughter was Ayşe's daughter-in-law, the one who had had her leg smashed up and lost her husband in the car-crash, so she was really one of the family, though with Fatma that didn't ensure that one was on good terms, rather the contrary. But here she was, ready and willing to do her best for a pretty bride.

Pembe's father then did the only thing he ever did for his daughter's wedding, he brought down eleven chairs from the tea-house for seat-ing. It wasn't enough and we hadn't a brazier to tune the *def* over, the vellum or whatever you call it gets baggy if it is not warmed every five minutes. But the guests who now began to come in made good these deficiencies. There was a water-tap in the corner and a couple of mugs; water is the only refreshment usually offered at the women's half of a wedding.

I had gone over to watch Hayriye putting the last touches to Pembe's make-up. They had borrowed the white crown with the silver tail from Ekrem's wife and Pembe was transformed. Zeynep and Hayriye looked after the bride—if it had been an English wedding they would have been called matrons of honour. The dancing was in full swing when they brought Pembe, in a red veil, over from Ayşe's house. Hayriye lifted the veil from her head when they were inside and led her to a place where she stood to receive the homage of the dancing, the best the women have to give. We all danced for her in turn and she kissed hands and we kissed hands. She wasn't Pembe any longer but a strange presence under the arches of my kitchen (Plate 10).

It was still cold in the crypt. A plump girl, the daughter of the hoca from the big mosque, was there and she felt the cold, so did Meryem, the cheery body from over the road. Then Zeynep's younger sister, Moazzez, came in. She teaches at the school in the nearby village where they love horses. Now she was in a plain green dress and danced with Pembe—Salim Hoca's daughter, a Kozankızı girl, danced with a Kaygısız girl, one who had been edged out of the Hacilar clan which had adopted her father. Moazzez is tall and fair; Salim Hoca has wonderful daughters.

Little girls danced, twiddling their skinny bodies and looking down at themselves with admiration. Little boys scrambled over the coal-pile at the back, murmured 'Look, she's throwing her navel.'

I sat on the stairs in the shadow and looked at Pembe round a pillar. She was shy of course, eyes downcast. Was she nervous? After all she was going to Ankara to live amongst strangers.

'Oooh, isn't it cold?' said someone shivering.

'Yes, and there are those men up at the teahouse drinking tea and smoking and soon they'll be back smelling like hoopoes. Let's go and put the henna on.' (I like that Turkish expression—I'd rather smell like a hoopoe than a polecat.)

'We can't for a bit, they've arranged for the bridegroom to come in and have his photo taken with Pembe and Zeynep and the rest.'

I'd been wriggling round through the crowd firing off that flash all the time. When İsmail did come shyly in I tried to shoo the women eager to be in the photo away from the background, but a Kaygısız wife slipped back, the wife of Abdullah the Curlew. He had had about five wives and though she was a cheery woman and a good housewife she didn't visit the Kaygısız much, they had grown tired of welcoming the Curlew's wives. So the group photo was a failure. But there were several of Pembe that were good. We had all put a dot of henna on our foreheads when Zeynep brought the ready-mixed bowlful in; a finger-tip dot like a caste-mark, for good fortune they said.

Fatma was still drumming away cheerfully when word was given that we were to go over to Ayşe's house for the henna ceremony. Back in her room Pembe slipped off the wedding dress and put on a salmon-pink nightie and negligé that İsmail had bought her, the nightie had a wide band of ruching round the hem and the coat part had it round the sleeves too. But she hadn't put the coat on when she came in for the henna, just swung it over her shoulders. She sat on a chair near the warmth of the stove and, putting her head in her hands, began to cry hopelessly. It was the first time I had seen her cry and I didn't know what to do. I stroked her wet cheek, Fatma sang her most sexy and laughter-provoking songs. But nothing was any good, she still cried, tears dripping on to the pink nightie.

Latife had the bowl of henna, now soft and well brewed. At last Pembe was persuaded to sit up and dry her wet hands and have some henna put on them. She only wanted it on the top joint of the little finger of her right hand, and Latife did it very very carefully, caressingly, making sure that every bit of skin and nail was covered by the henna within the chosen area, stopping sharply at a line encircling the finger at the joint. There were old soft rags ready to hold it in place, and a strip was torn and tied neatly round the finger. Then her toes were done, again very slowly and carefully and neatly, and wrapped, one foot at a time, and her pink slippers put on again. Fatma had started dancing herself, astonishingly well, her flabby old body balancing beautifully between her uplifted hands, light and lovely as a ballet dancer.

We all went to bed. They told me to come round at half-past eight or nine, the bus would arrive then for all the furniture to be loaded on it to go to Ankara.

In the morning the snow had held off and there was a clear sky for the sun to rise into. I was to be the driver and responsible should a tyre-change be needed or any other emergency arise, as İsmail would be in his best new suit, so I put on cord trousers, a thick sweater and a sheepskin jacket. The sun was dazzling over the eastern slope of the

Nar valley and there was just a little dry, powdery snow to brush off the car.

The others were at breakfast in Latife's house where İsmail had slept. There was a dish of hot fried mince on the cloth on the floor, and the new bread and tea; I ate well. Ayşe just had a glass of tea since she had had stomach pains all the week and feared an ulcer. She had been going up to the health officer for the village remedy of shots of something or other, but probably it was nerves; she would be all right when Pembe was safely settled.

Hayriye then took Pembe into the sleeping-room at Ayşe's house, where the stove had been kept lit all night, and helped her put on the wedding dress again, with all the make-up. The hair-spray had worked well and her coiffure was fine. Outside in Ayşe's yard Zeynep was supervising the loading of the furniture on to the roof of the bus. Chair after chair, huge bundles wrapped in old *kilims*, it all went somewhere.

Şevket appeared suddenly.

'It's all right, all right,' he said eagerly, 'the marriage registrar has come back from his holidays. We are all to go up now and get it done.'

İsmail and Pembe and Şevket piled into my car to drive to the municipal building on the Meydan. There the bride and groom got out like royalty and went up the steps to sit at the table in the office, opposite the registrar. Then the registrar stood up, and we all stood too, while he made the usual little speech, wishing them good fortune. They sat down again, Pembe, I was glad to see, graceful and straight. She signed her name firmly and legibly in the book and so did İsmail. Then there was a hitch, each must supply a photograph. They said they had some in Ankara and Şevket said he would bring them to the office as soon as possible. Then we all processed back to the car again and returned to the house where the loading was still in progress. A crowd of watchers had gathered, women on the side of the street by the bus, men on the other.

The stepmother was standing by Ayşe's gate, desperately opening and shutting her eyes in an effort to squeeze some tears into them, because it is the right thing for mothers to cry at weddings. But no tears would come. Pembe's father was across the road with the men. I'm glad they watched. Her father looked expressionless but worried as usual.

Pembe wasn't crying either. I was thankful the weather was fine and we could go in the little Volkswagen. Ayşe was going with us, she couldn't face staying in the empty house and she hoped her son Mehmet, whom she planned to visit for a week or two, might take her to a doctor who would cure her stomach. Pembe was standing by the gate with her head up, as proud as a queen. The newly risen sun glittered on the lace and embroidery of her bridal gown and on the crisp snow. She was looking long and steadily at the old Hacilar house, plainly visible between the bare boughs of the disputed mulberry grove.

I too was going to stay the night at Mehmet's house and pushed a toothbrush and nightie into the car. Ayşe sat beside me in front and the other two at the back, hardly talking, each shy in a corner. To break the ice I told them they would be able to hold hands happily there at the back. But İsmail was furious at that, I had hurt his pride. Of course he wouldn't hold his bride's hand in public. Frightened, I apologized for my incivility, said I was ignorant, our customs in England were different. And it was all right. They went on sitting in their corners, chatting sometimes shyly, like a boy and girl at their first dance.

On we went through the frosty brilliant sunshine, past the ancient dead craters, through a village where children and donkeys were scattered all over the road as usual. Why not? It was an unusual day only for us.

On over the hill road, the hills golden brown under the light snow, clear in the pure air, the only trace of habitation a little village or two of humble, square mud houses.

Over the highest part of the road and there on the southern horizon was a conical white mountain, Hasan Dağ.

Where our road joined the main highway we stopped for petrol. The attendant didn't look into the car, kept his eyes down as I handed him the money, apologized, bowed to the bride as to royalty.

On again, along six-mile straights ended only by rises in the road. Flocks of cranes and of mute swans, with the characteristic black bump on their faces, lifted over the road, flew over our heads and touched down like planes on the brown arable far to the right. Gliding and swooping, it was hard to see their colour against the blue sky and the white snow. Birds to greet Pembe sitting in her corner. She glanced at the eagles parading along the road edge, perching on tele-graph poles, big reddish birds with striped heads and a lovely pattern of light and dark on their underwings. On and on in the clear air and brilliant sunshine of the plateau in winter, the Salt Lake crumpled into lively blue ripples on our left.

'Are you hungry?' asked İsmail. We stopped at the restaurant by the Konya fork, and İsmail instructed me to go right over to the far edge of the parking area, looking over the empty fields. He got out and fetched tea and a loaf filled with meat. We nibbled a bit, except for Pembe, and drank our tea. The boy fetched the glasses, bowing humbly and not looking into the car.

On for the last hundred kilometres, past the Gölbaşi lake which was frozen a queer matt-grey colour, with straight white ridges running across it like bulging cracks where the pressure of expanding ice had forced the huge slabs up; here and there melt-water in still pools mirrored the snowy hills on the other side. Into Ankara we went, along the fine streets of the Yenimahalle suburb.

'Stop at that green gate,' ordered İsmail.

I stopped, got out, lifted my seat to let them both out. They went up the garden path past the little fir tree and disappeared into their house.

Then İsmail came back and led us in proudly. He went into a room with Pembe while we looked round the rest of the house. It was lovely, absolutely bare and clean and full of sunshine. So Zeynep had managed to clean it and still get down to Nar on the same day as İsmail. A bathroom with a lavatory beyond it, a small Turkish bath-room with a water heater and a drain. There was a spare room at the north side which would be cool in summer, and could be used either as a guest-room or for sitting in. And the kitchen, with İsmail's one bachelor glass and plate, knife and fork and spoon. In the corner, a great earthenware jar with a wooden cover, full of icy spring water, the kind sold in Ankara in glass carboys because there is chlorine in the tap water and it is thought undrinkable.

Then they came out and joined us; we said how clean it was and İsmail said he had kept it nice, Zeynep had not had to do much, that was why she had been able to get away so soon. We found a cupboard full of firewood with some splinters of pine on the top to light it with, and we soon had the stove going: he had put it in the middle of the little hall to warm both the bedroom and sitting-room. And we relaxed and rested; we didn't know how long the bus would be with Zeynep and the rest of them and the furniture. The sun shone into the empty rooms. It was perfect. I smiled at Pembe, thinking 'Today put on perfection . . .' but I couldn't translate it. Did Pembe look nervous? She was standing about, a bit tense. But we were innocent as children, full of goodwill to each other and to humanity.

The bus came after a couple of hours and pulled up at the green gate. Everything was unloaded and brought in very quickly, plenty of willing hands helped and I tried to keep out of the way, as Pembe certainly did, very properly. The brownish-red armchairs, four of them and a sofa, fitted perfectly into the south room, and a sea-green Isparta carpet, the gift of Neziha, went down in the middle, exactly the right size. İsmail's friend fussed over the business of putting the glass buffet İsmail had bought in Nevşehir against one wall.

Zeynep was in charge in the bedroom. A big bedstead was piled with bedding, topped with embroidered cushions. She tried first one bedspread, then another. She hadn't been to her own house yet, it was five minutes' walk away. The *yolluk* was a bit long for the passage from the door, but we got it down somehow, they fitted it better later. Zeynep's husband went out and bought food, fresh loaves and cheese and olives, blessed foods all of them, and we sat on the bedroom floor and ate, Pembe standing by the door and only nibbling. She tied and untied the lace girdle of her dress, it was all crumpled.

'That girdle is looking all dirty and spoiling the dress,' I said. 'Why don't you take it off? It would look much better without it.'

'Oh, I can't possibly do that, only İsmail can do that tonight.'

Again I felt silly and ignorant.

Two big shapes in heavy overcoats were visible through the net curtains of the window. İsmail went to let them in; it was his brother from Erzurum with a friend. Şevket sat in the new guest-room with them and heard the news. İsmail's mother had come from Erzurum with the brother, they hadn't known when the wedding was to be, or exactly where, and had been staying with his sister and her husband in Ankara, the parents of the lad who had come down with İsmail to Nar. Soon his mother herself arrived, with all the rest of the family, eager to see the new bride.

The big old woman came quietly into the house, Pembe came out of the bedroom and kissed her hand, then she kissed Pembe on both cheeks and Pembe retired again into the bedroom. The splendid old thing went on into the sitting-room and sat down. People were sitting everywhere, on the arms of the new chairs and on the floor. They admired the glass buffet with the greeny-blue coffee set in it. After Zeynep and Mehmet and I, and of course Ayşe, had made the acquaintance of the newcomers, had shown ourselves to be present and correct, we left Pembe with her new family and went down and had tea and sausage in Zeynep's house. But something had been worrying Pembe, she had cried again as she said goodbye to us. Then it all came out, she had made Zeynep promise to go straight back there, perhaps for the night, at any rate for the first part of the night. She told me Pembe's mother had nearly bled to death on her wedding night and they were all frightened it might run in the family. So that was it. I never thought. How deep did it go? Was that why she had worked so hard at school, to put off the thought of marriage as long as she could? They went out. Ayşe and I sat by the stove.

About nine they got back with good news, everything was all right. Now we could sleep.

Next day I planned to go back to Nar. Ayşe said she would stay for a week or two to see a doctor. The first thing to do before I left was to visit Pembe and her new family. I put on a dress with a good diamond brooch and went up to her house with Zeynep and Ayşe.

There was her mother-in-law sitting by the stove as though she owned the place, as of course she did according to their custom. Pembe greeted us, smiling, the grand hair-do all washed out and her hair bound close in a white head-scarf.

I sat on a cushion on the floor beside the stove, on one side of the old lady. I said Zeynep was our Hoca's daughter and what a good man he was. Even I, a Christian, could see that. She said she had come from Serbia when she was twenty-six, with six young children, and all their friends in Serbia had been Christian.

Zeynep brought out all the different piles of underwear in their pink wrappers and presented them on her knees, looking up at Pembe's new mother as she did so, her wide grey eyes smiling with innocent serenity. She told me later that she wouldn't have given them at all if Ismail's mother hadn't bothered to come to the wedding. The lady spoke with great dignity, saying that they didn't mind about all those things, what they were interested in was people. But she was obviously glad that everything was given correctly.

I saw them again, I helped Pembe with some debts outstanding on the furniture; I told her how much she had pleased me by letting me do something that St. Nicholas had done, a great saint from the west of Turkey who had helped young girls with their dowries. As I talked to the old lady I saw Pembe kneeling at her prayer ritual in the shadows of the bedroom. She had really found a mother, she had love and security, the things she had been looking for.

I returned to Nar after the wedding; women surrounded the car, Fadime, Meryem, several others . . . and the stepmother, shouting in my ear:

'Pembe's father could not sleep last night, could not sleep. He feared Pembe was too small . . . too small . . . too small. How is she? How is she? Small . . . Small.'

She'd a voice like a corncrake. Thoughtful now that Pembe's out of the way, I thought unkindly.

'Pembe's fine, absolutely all right. Her new mother is a very good woman. She loves Pembe.'

And they went back to their houses to spread the news.

'Pembe is very well, Pembe is very well.'

CONCLUSION

The mountain cone blocks the setting sun. All the wheat has been cut and stacked.

Mediha, a thick-set plain girl, laughs as she bends to pick up the narrow-necked water-jar, then takes it with her into the vineyard, where she washes her ears, her face, hands, arms and hair, looping her veil out free over her shoulders. She prays, bending, kneeling, straightening again, her hands crossed on her breast.

She gets on the cart with the white horse, belonging to her mother, Haci Baba's eldest daughter, and goes home to the village.

Snow lies frozen in the corners of her father's court. Women sit close around a little room, the air hot from the small stove, women two deep on the window seat, women on the floor. Mediha sits by her mother, her face radiant.

'Yes, I am going to be married. Look, he gave me these gold medallions, fifteen of them. These big, old ones with Arabic lettering are worth twice as much as the others, see how they shine, the polish of the old pure gold.'

'I saw him here last Sunday evening, spoke with him, held his hand.'

'Yes, he is good,' said everyone. 'He has land, gardens. He is good.'

'You must take photographs of all of us,' says Gülten, 'all of us, even the new lamb.'

The girls crowd together in the snow, beautifying the bride, touching her hair, their own flowing down their backs.

'Let's put all the gold on the lamb and take its picture,' say the girls.

'No,' says little Mehmet, 'take me and my dog.'

Mehmet is lonely, it is the bride's day.

She stands arrayed, ready with God's care and in agreement with his will to support the responsibility of being the mother of her husband's children, the mother of men who will continue to cultivate the lands of Nar.

Sun on snow. The bridegroom leads his bride up the hill to where a dwelling has been prepared in a corner of his father's court, leads her veiled in red through the deep snow between the rows of watching children, to where his mother is waiting to salute her. Then he sets Mediha in his house, like a flower, like a tree.

In Nar life goes on.

Priest Weston
1973

NOTE ON LOCAL GOVERNMENT
IN RURAL TURKEY

Turkey is governed by the Ministry of the Interior, *İçişleri Bakanlığı*. *Vali* and *Kaymakam* are the chief officials of the Ministry in the provinces. A *Vali* governs a Province or *Vilayet*, of which there are sixty-six in Turkey. The *Vilayet* of Nevşehir includes five towns or *Kaza*, each of which is ruled by a Town Governor or *Kaymakam*. All the provinces are so divided into five or six towns, so a *Kaymakam* is very much lower in the hierarchy than a *Vali*, though both must have a good degree in Political Science or Law. A *Kaymakam* may become a *Vali* if he stays in the Ministry until he is sufficiently senior. He is independent in decisions and judgements within his *kaza*, though he reports to his *Vali* regularly. He is responsible for co-ordinating education, health service, law, police and road construction, and for seeing that work in these and other departments goes on as it should. Anyone, man or woman, may seek audience of a *Kaymakam* without appointment and he will right their wrongs, or, if that is not possible, make their position clear in a friendly and thoughtful way.

For a vivid account of the troubles between an idealistic young *Kaymakam* and big business, see Yaşar Kemal's short story, 'The Drumming Out', in Turkish '*Teneke*', the tin can, which presumably was fastened to the car which took the *Kaymakam* away when the greedy rice magnates achieved his dismissal.

NOTE ON MUSICAL INSTRUMENTS
IN THE VILLAGE OF NAR

Def A *def* cannot be bought, it is the women's instrument and women do not traditionally handle money. To make one, take a ring of thin wood fifteen inches across and four or five inches deep. The wooden ring of an old sieve will do. When you (or your neighbour) slaughter a cow for meat, take the skin of the biggest stomach and clean it well; stretch a piece of it over your wooden ring while the skin is still damp, and smooth it tightly down over the sides. When it is dry you may play on it, drumming with your finger-tips, but first it may need to be warmed over a brazier until the skin is taut and its sound when tapped is ringing and resonant. Sing to it, lively earthy songs with a twist to them.

Saz A *saz* is a stringed instrument of great beauty used to accompany love songs. It is played by a man who rests the long-necked shining tasselled instrument across his knees as he sits. It has a smallish soundbox shaped like that of a mandolin and is strung so as to produce notes of great density and richness. It is played with plectrum or fingers; Big Mehmet who built the wheat mill is one of the best *saz* players in Nar. A *saz* costs from £3 to £15.

Kaval The shepherd's pipe, on which some village lads are very skilful.

Davul The big drum. One of the drumsticks used to play it is shaped like a small wooden scimitar. It is used to wake the people in the nights of Ramazan, and, with a trumpet-ended *zurna* or clarinet, is played by men at their comrades' weddings.

Keman The violin. A gipsy instrument used to accompany their dance, the *köçek*.

GLOSSARY

abla: elder sister; a polite way of addressing a woman not too much older than the speaker.

ağabey: elder brother; also a polite way of addressing a man, even a total stranger, not younger than the speaker. Common spelling *abi.*

aleikum selam: response to the greeting *selamun aleikum,* q.v.

bağ: vineyard.

bayram: festival, religious or state.

beygir: a stallion, as are all Nar horses.

bulgur: wheat which has been boiled, dried and cracked.

çarşaf: ordinary white sheet, used to put on a bed, to veil a woman in the street, or to wrap a corpse for burial.

cezve: a tiny coffee saucepan.

çıkacak: public display of the dowry and gifts a bride is taking to her new home.

dağ: mountain.

darbuka: a small drum.

def: a very big tambourine played by women.

dimi: wide cotton trousers worn by women, of plain rectangular shape with holes for the feet.

dink: an upright millstone which revolves on a platform, similar in appearance to a Herefordshire cider mill, but used to crack wheat.

gecekondu: 'built at night'; squatters' quarter of a city.

gelin: a bride; she will be called 'our *gelin*' by her husband's family all her life. The word means 'come' and she has come to them.

gelincik: red field poppy, *papaver rheas.*

gunah: an ordinary sin, difficult to avoid, such as not to pray regularly or (for women) to let a curl of hair slip out from beneath the headveil.

hanım: lady, used after the first name in respectfully speaking to or of a lady you know. *Sevinç,* meaning joy, is a common name in Nar and I was usually called Sevinç Hanım or Sevinç *abla* in Nar.

haram: an unthinkable and impossible sin, completely forbidden, like eating pork.

helva: a sweetmeat sold in shops in large cream-and-brown blocks, made from the seeds of sesame, a plant grown commercially in south Turkey.

hoca: teacher, especially a religious teacher attached to a mosque, but used in addressing lycée and middle school teachers, e.g. Nesrin Hoca.

iftar: the ceremonial meal which breaks the fast each evening of Ramazan.

ikram: refreshment such as coffee which must be offered to a guest.

kandil: lights which adorn the balconies of minarets on holy nights.

kilim: tapestry-weave rug without pile, of ancient and geometric design.

köçek: a gipsy dance performed by a male entertainer dressed in a full skirt.

köfte: rissole made with minced lamb, onion and parsley patted into a leaf shape and then fried. Eaten cold on picnics.

koftır: a sweetmeat made from grape sugar boiled down until thick, thickened with wheat starch and dried in the sun.

lakap: ancient village clan or lineage.

masallar (pl.): fairy tales, often ancient, told by women to children.

mihrab: tall, narrow green-painted niche inside a mosque; indicates the direction of Mecca so that worshippers may face that way.

moda: the fashion, fashion magazine.

müdür: a director; the title given to the head of a school, bank, business or similar concern.

muhtar: headman chosen by the elders of the village to deal with the Government, to find markets for crops they wish to sell and to arrange for the supply of necessities such as winter coal.

navruz: the spring equinox when the Persians celebrate the New Year; a little iris which comes into bloom about 22 March.

pazarlık: bargaining in its everyday use, but in referring to wedding ceremonial it means a party between engagement and wedding at which a dress and nightdress are cut out.

pide: a soft, flat loaf leavened with old dough and baked by the baker in a brick oven in time for breakfast every day; it may be plain, or be rolled round cheese and parsley before baking, or be baked flat with meat and tomato spread on top like a pizza.

pilau: rice or bulgur cooked with fat, onions and tomatoes, very light if properly prepared. The English spelling is pilaff.

sahur: the meal taken before dawn during Ramazan.

şalvar: full trousers shaped a little to the leg, worn by men and women. More usual in the south than in Nar. They may be made of wool, cotton or silk.

selah: ritual announcement from the minaret on the occasion of a death or an eclipse of the moon.

selamun aleikum: Muslim greeting meaning 'Peace be upon you'; the response *aleikum selam* means the same.

sunnet: a practice enjoined by religious custom, usually meaning circumcision; the use of henna on the hands and hair of women is also *sunnet.*

tandır: a yard-wide thirty-inch deep pit, near a house and covered by a roof, in which a fire is lit to cook *yufka* (q.v.) or beans in earthenware jars, the *tandır fasulya* which is a famous Nar dish.

tay: a colt.

testi: a narrow-necked earthenware water-jar, holding about a gallon. All those used in Nar were made by potters at Avanos twenty kilometres to the north, by the Red River. (Kızıl Irmak).

trampet: small flattish drum slung horizontally round the neck and played with two drumsticks.

yerli: the local peasant aristocracy to whom the land belongs, though none in Nar have large holdings.

yolluk: a long, narrow rug to cover the floor of a passage in a house.

yufka: paper-thin unleavened bread made in yard-wide circular sheets and cooked on a circle of sheet-iron over a *tandır.*